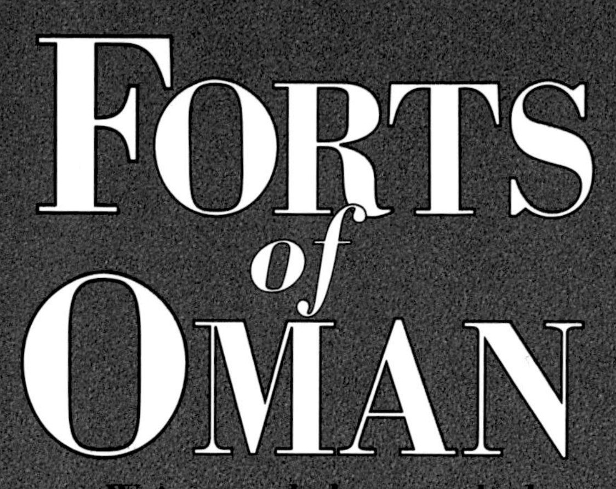

Written and photographed
by Walter Dinteman

Published by
Motivate Publishing

PO Box 2331
Dubai, UAE
Tel: (04) 824060
Fax: (04) 824436

PO Box 43072
Abu Dhabi, UAE
Tel: (02) 311666
Fax: (02) 311888

London House
26/40, Kensington High Street
London W8 4PF
Tel: (071) 938 2222
Fax: (071) 937 7293

Directors:
Obaid Humaid Al Tayer
Ian Fairservice

Senior Editor: Julia Roles
Deputy Editor: Ann Verbeek
Art Director: Mark Pettipher
Layout Artist: Karen Coutinho

British Library Cataloguing-in-Publication
Data. A catalogue record for this book is
available from the British Library.

First published 1993

ISBN 1 873544 41 3

Printed by:
Emirates Printing Press, Dubai

Cover and title page: The imposing fort at Nakhl.
Inside cover pages: The ceiling of one of the main rooms of Rustaq Castle Fort is decorated with geometric designs which reflect an African influence.
Contents page and chapter openers: Evening silhouettes of fortifications at Al Khawd, Mutrah, Fateh and Fanja.

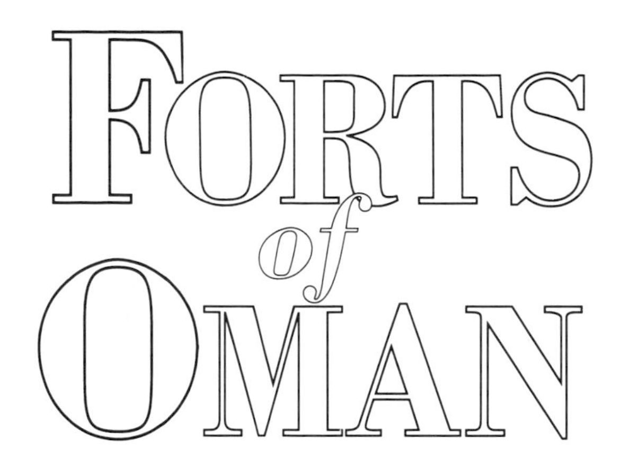

Forts of Oman

Published with the support
and encouragement of
مشاريع خط الصحراء ش.م.م

Contents

INTRODUCTION

Widespread throughout Oman, forts and watchtowers add a picturesque element to the country's landscape. Forts crown rocky outcrops overlooking ancient harbours, they cling to cliffs above wadis, and straddle craggy peaks throughout the interior. Some rise majestically above a village and its palm groves, while others are decaying, their skeletons forming sad, ghostly silhouettes against the setting sun. Formed by violent earth plate movements more than a hundred million years ago, the mountain areas of Oman provide a stark backdrop to the county's fortifications. Smooth-surfaced buildings and towers stand out from the rugged backgrounds of red, sienna, umber, grey and green rock surfaces.

Arab expansion into Europe and North Africa during the 7th and 8th centuries was rapid and on a large scale. It became practical for them to take over existing buildings and employ local craftsmen to construct new domestic quarters in the lands they conquered. The gradual absorption and interchange of indigenous cultures helped to assimilate various designs and architectural elements into an Islamic design.

By the 8th century, Muslim world frontiers had been established and a system of defence was defined. Military protection was initially centred on fortified cities. Two types of military installations dominated: single forts located outside major settlements, and walled communities.

As central authority weakened in the 9th and 10th centuries, local dynasties took over, frequently fighting each other. Oman was no exception. In Oman, as in the rest of the Arab world, this caused the spread of military architecture to every urban centre. Fortified walls, mighty towers and elaborate gates became the norm for most towns after the 10th century. The walls and towers were massive constructions built with local materials: mud brick at Bahla; stone and mortar in Mudairib. Round, square and elongated towers served as buttresses, lodgings and arsenals. Crenellations, walkways, machicolations and small protective cupolas, located at various wall sections, were stock elements in the construction of Omani fort walls and towers.

Many large buildings had gun ports for defence, thus most dwellings were built as fortifications. Fortified houses and communal structures were necessary for tribal security. Entrance to Omani houses was usually through a single doorway within an elaborate door or gate. The buildings within an Omani city's walls were one-, two- and three-storey, flat-roofed constructions, with no windows on the street side.

Military forts protected seaports, and were the guardians of trade routes. They were also a base for tribal conflicts. Powerful Imams resided in castle forts, reflecting their influence and wealth. Smaller forts and aswar provided refuge for villagers under attack by foreign forces or warring tribes. Some forts were combined with walled cities, such as forts Mirani and Jalali, in Muscat.

Oman's forts are Arabic in design, built by Omanis with Persian and Portuguese influences. Today they remain in various forms of preservation, dominating the Omani landscape. Forts generally consisted of a walled enclosure with or without towers or bastions. Secondary defences consisted of isolated watchtowers. This concentric system is said to be of Arabic origin, and the concept was taken back and adopted in Europe by soldiers returning from the Crusades.

Military and castle forts are imposing and structurally substantial. Repeated repairs and modifications have enabled them to survive for many centuries. Forts similar to those at Bahla, Nakhl, Nizwa and Rustaq, once formed the military and political centre of a province, and were built to dominate as well as to protect the surrounding countryside.

Most forts have played an important part in Oman's history of domestic wars, both tribal and dynastic, and numerous battles fought against foreign aggressors. At one point in this history, the Persians were called upon by one tribe to assist in their conflict against another tribe. Once they had a foothold in Oman, the Persians attempted to take control of the entire country. Warring tribes then combined forces to expel them.

Oman has long been a seafaring nation, prospering by its position on the trade route between China, India and East Africa. The Arabs from remote ages have navigated the seas between Africa and India, using scientific instruments and producing charts of voyages as far afield as China and Malaysia. An Omani sailor, Ahmed bin Majid, was navigator to Vasco da Gama on his journey to the Orient in 1498. This journey permitted the Portuguese to establish a trade monopoly with the Far East which they then dominated for the next 150 years.

An event having a great impact on Oman occurred a long distance from its shores. Portugal appointed Afonso d'Albuquerque to the position of Viceroy of India. In 1507, he secured the East African coast and captured several strategic Middle Eastern locations, including Muscat, in order to protect the Portuguese sea trade routes. Between 1507 and 1650, Portugal controlled the commercial traffic of the Indian Ocean, and Muscat became an important supply base with forts protecting its harbour. An enemy

Right: Part of the time-ravaged mud-brick fort at Bahla.

controlling Muscat could seriously impede the flow of Portuguese commerce. The Portuguese also captured Sur, Barka, Mutrah and Sohar, thus controlling the entire Omani coast along the Gulf of Oman. However, they never penetrated the interior, due to the hostility of the Omanis combined with the impenetrable Jebel Akhdar mountain range.

An important factor regarding forts at this time was the introduction of gunpowder into warfare. Gunpowder, consisting of sulphur, saltpeter and charcoal, was first used in battle in 1325 AD. Techniques had become refined enough by the 15th century to make guns a serious weapon.

The Monsmeg gun, now in Edinburgh Castle, cast in 1449 for the Duke of Burgundy, was able to fire an iron ball for 1,250 metres and a stone ball for 2,600 metres. In the 15th century the Portuguese were aware that the Turks had captured Constantinople with the aid of cannon, and this influenced their design of the forts in Muscat. Square towers were replaced by round towers, better to deflect cannon shot. But large cannons were difficult to manhandle, so to improve firing mobility, the arqebus, a hand-held gun, was introduced as a principal infantry weapon. This muzzle-loading gun gave the Portuguese an immediate advantage over local populations fighting with traditional weapons. It was simple in construction, had a long life, and was soon adopted by local militia who quickly mastered the techniques of its construction. Omani musketeers and gunners soon became prominent in warfare.

When the Portuguese occupied Muscat in 1507, they were immediately aware of Omani hostility. Thus they chose the most commanding places atop rocky outcrops for the building of forts Mirani, Jalali and Mutrah. This strategic planning reinforced the superb natural defences of Muscat.

The Portuguese assembled pre-fabricated forts in the African Gold Coast areas they possessed. A typical fort-building expedition would include three ships with 500 soldiers, 100 masons and a complete fort with numbered stones and doors ready for assembly-by-numbers. Portuguese military architecture, influenced by Italian architectural practice, gave way in Muscat to the need for immediate secure positions. The emphasis was on natural defence rather than on the building of massive military structures. With its natural disposition of bastions, the forts of Muscat were simple in their planning and bore little

Right: In the vicinity of Muscat, many watchtowers like these at Saal provided protection for the villages and terraced palm groves.

relationship to the standards of military architecture of the period. The pre-fabricated fort usually referred to by the Portuguese for overseas construction, was abandoned in Muscat in favour of independent architectural structures. These new constructions developed a regional characteristic. An individual design resulted from the fact that the mountain-top position of the Omani forts became a more important factor in their defensive usefulness, than adhering to an established Portuguese design. Certainly the layout of Fort Capitan, later Fort Mirani, was dictated by the necessity to build a fort quickly, and there was not enough time to produce a more traditional fort plan. A second factor was the constant shortage of skilled personnel, which resulted in the forts being built by local craftsmen, who, using their indigenous technology, left their own indelible mark on the architecture. However, following the 1581 attack on Muscat by the Turkish admiral, Ali Beg, the Portuguese did enlist the help of their old mentors, and in 1586 an Italian architect was sent from Milan to rebuild Fort Mirani.

Forts varied in size from large, grandiose structures like the Palace of Imam Bil'arub, now called Jabrin Castle Fort, to a simple walled rectangular sur.

'Noble', 'monumental', 'a ruler's residence', 'unique architectural designs', 'beautiful decorations with artistic Islamic inscriptions' are but a few descriptions applied to a castle fort. Unlike the compact, austere quarters of a military fort, such as Al Hazm, the castle fort's interior was palatial. Military forts were often occupied by Walis and Imams but they were built principally for military

purposes. Castle forts, on the other hand, were built for comfortable living, but had to be fort-like for defensive purposes. Some castle forts, like Jabrin and Birkat Al Mauz, housed the government. Others such as Bait Na'man and Al Hobe were used as retreats and rest-houses for travellers doing the several days' camel trip from Muscat to Nizwa or Sohar.

A sur was used as a temporary shelter by a number of people, their belongings and animals. In Oman, the Arabic term 'sur' means 'walled area'. Unlike a castle fort or fortified house, the sur was not the property of a single family but was built and maintained by a tribe for communal use in the event of enemy approaches.

In his study 'The Sur of the Batinah', Dr Paolo Costa reported that there were about ninety such fortifications stretched along the several hundred kilometres of farmland between Muscat and Shinas.

In the early days of Omani settlement, when a tribe was threatened by a neigbouring or distant enemy, it found protection at the top of a hill. The Batinah Plain is flat and did not offer settlers to the area protection from their aggressors. To a large extent this determined the location and architecture of sur construction. Aswar (plural for sur) built on flat land were surrounded by either a dry moat or a second wall. Many were simple walled enclosures with a single fortified entrance. Depending on the size of the sur, various defensive elements like towers, sentry

Below: Nakhl Fort was considered invulnerable by the Omanis, who had a deep sense of its military strength.

walks and machicolations were added. Living quarters and sometimes a keep may have been built, but these buildings never became permanent dwellings. Villagers would retreat to these aswar during the threat of attack by a foreign enemy or during inter-tribal friction.

In the Batinah region there are too many aswar to be covered in this book. The selected aswar were chosen as examples of variations on the square enclosure with two diagonally opposite towers (see floor plans on page 131), and to show the various stages of their preservation. Time,

and the effects of weathering and expanding communities are taking their toll on the aswar. Some are now merely mounds of earth others have remnants of walls and crumbling towers.

Ruins are not as pretty as the restored forts, but they have an aura of ancient times. Also, one can roam around within them and see the remains of walls dividing rooms, of parapets where sentries once stood and of angled entryways. The restored aswar are generally locked so that viewing is limited to the exterior of walls and towers.

Forts protected the towns and populated areas while aswar provided retreats for people of farming and fishing villages. Watchtowers had a different defensive mission. They were outposts to protect inland trade routes and to guard water supplies. They served as look-out towers from which, at the sight of invaders,

Left: The ends of wooden rungs were set into the walls of towers and forts to provide access to the crenellations.
Below: Al Felaij Fort, near Barka, was restored in 1990.

warning shots could alert the garrison at a nearby fort. Some towers were adjacent to forts, where they formed a secondary defence, and were rallying points, permitting the besieged to make sorties under cover of artillery fire. There were watchtowers with a single, but attached, fortified room, similar to the one on the outskirts of Nizwa, in which several families could seek refuge during a period of danger.

"As we passed the outlying watchtowers commanding the various approaches, the guards therein fired their matchlocks to give warning, which was soon responded to by the thunder of the guns of the fort." So quoted an early 19th-century traveller on approaching Nizwa. The watchtower was serving its purpose, as the focal point of a defensive system based on the concentration of a small number of defenders against numerous attackers, to warn of approaching strangers, friendly or hostile.

Until the 'modernisation' of Oman in 1972, permission was required from tribal leaders to pass through tribal territory. It was customary, when moving from one part of Oman to another, to take a ghafir (protector or guide) or two, from each of the tribes through whose country one was passing. This applied to Arabs, as well as strangers, as an Arab sometimes needed to pass through an area controlled by a tribe with whom his tribe was not in good standing.

The architecture of watchtowers is more variable than that of forts. Some towers are tall slim structures, while others are short and squat. Tall towers increased the range of the guns. Towers large in diameter were needed for cannon, allowing space for gun recoil and for firing more than one gun at a time.

Watchowers also vary in the texture of materials used. Some have a stone-and-mortar base with a mud-brick top section and others are made solely from mud-brick. Entrances are equally variable. A small door at ground level requires one to crawl into the tower. Wood or stone rungs projecting from the side of a tower's wall lead, like stairs, to a door half-way up its side. A ladder or palm log gives entrance to another tower, while some require a certain amount of dexterity, by climbing a rope suspended from a slit in the wall. Loopholes were located on the floor beneath the cannon, permitting musketeers to defend against an enemy approaching close to the tower where cannon fire was ineffectual.

Many travellers in old Oman moved about with a camel safari, carrying tents, water, food and gifts; accompanied by ghafar and a number of armed men for protection against raiding parties. Such was the make-up of an early 19th century party approaching Buraimi, as described by one of its members: "...just as it was getting dusk, arrived at our destination, ... a small hamlet of about 100 souls. The sudden appearance of a mounted party, evidently well-armed, threw the good people into a ferment, and in their excitement the guard in the watchtower greeted us with a volley from their matchlocks. We were so near at the time that one of the bullets grazed a camel's leg, but no harm was done; and as such incidents were too common to be noticed, we were soon seated amicably in the midst of the elders, who expressed regret for their precipitation."

The highest concentration of watchtowers in Oman is along the main mountain passageways from the coast of Oman to the interior. These are Wadi Samail – from Muscat to Izki; Wadi Jizzi – from Sohar to Buraimi; and Wadi Hawasinah – from Al Khabura to Ibri. Although Wadi Awabi, Wadi Fulaij and Wadi Sahtan are not routes right through the mountains, they are included as good examples of watchtower distribution. Watchtowers were also built on the flat plains, as exemplified in the Dhahirah and Sharqiyah regions.

With the accession of His Majesty Sultan Qaboos bin Said Al Said in 1970, and the renaissance of Oman as a modern, prosperous state, the military and castle forts, watchtowers, aswar and other city fortifications punctuating the landscape, took on a different perspective. No longer important strongholds, they suddenly became monuments to a period that had changed overnight.

The government of Oman considers forts to be symbols of the greatness of Oman's past. Recently, several major forts have been restored by the Ministry of National Heritage and Culture, and more are scheduled for restoration. Traditional materials are being used: mud bricks, palm fronds, logs, Omani gypsum and limestone. Methods used in the building of the original structure are being followed to retain the colour and texture of the original fort.

To understand the role of forts in Omani heritage, we need to go back in history to look at the times when defensive structures were a necessity. This book attempts to show, by means of photographic and historical sketches, how the multitude of forts and towers, seemingly isolated, are related through history, politics, construction techniques and design.

Left: An askari guards the main gates of the fort at Rustaq. Below: Traditional materials being used in the restoration of Bait Na'man Castle Fort.

FORTS OF OMAN

FORT MIRANI

Two forts were built in Muscat – Fort Capitan (Mirani) and Fort Jaoa (Jalali) – and one in Mutrah. Fort Capitan was built by Don Manuel da Souza Coutinho in 1507, whose name is engraved in a stone tablet over one of the entrances. Fort Mirani was the first in Oman to use the new science of cannonarchy. When the Turks used heavy cannon to breach the walls of Constantinople in 1453, the Portuguese quickly saw the value of heavy artillery, and this influenced their building of heavily fortified bastions. This may account for Fort Mirani probably having more cannon than any other fort of its time.

During the expansion of the Ottoman Empire from Turkey and Egypt, Turkish admirals Piri Reis and Ali Beg attacked Muscat twice, in 1550 and 1581. These were only temporary setbacks for the Portuguese and they were able to re-establish their authority.

An Italian architect, C B Cairate, was sent from Milan in 1586 to rebuild the forts of Muscat. In the 1500s, Italy had become prominent in the field of military architecture, and by means of new forms and design, the school of Italian Architect Engineers influenced the whole field of European fortifications.

When the Portuguese lost the port of Hormuz (opposite the Musandam Peninsula) to the Persians in 1622, Muscat became their major naval base in the Gulf area. Muscat's forts were strengthened as defence against the Persians. By this time, however, Portuguese power had begun to decline. In 1650 Sultan bin Saif I captured forts Mirani, Jalali and Mutrah from the Portuguese after a long siege. Notwithstanding the bravery of the Omanis, the fall of Fort Mirani was due mainly to intrigue involving the governor.

In *A New Account of the East Indies* (1727), Alexander Hamilton tells of the Omani onslaught against the Portuguese: "The Portuguese flanked them, from their forts on the mountains, with plenty of great and small shot; but the Arabs never looked back, nor minded the great numbers of their dead companions, but mounted the walls over the carcasses of their slain... In the attack on the town [of Muscat], the Arabs lost between 4,000 and 5,000 of the best of their forces; and the Portuguese in their forts were reduced to 60 or 70... Those in the great fort [Mirani] held out about six months, under great want and fatigue; and all hope of relief being cut off, they resolved on a surrender, on which motion the impudent Governor, who was the sole cause of their calamity, leapt down a precipice into the sea where, the water being very shallow, he was dashed to pieces on the rocks..."

Except for a few conflicts, Fort Mirani's cannons were used mainly for saluting visiting ships or firing warning shots at ships attempting to enter the harbour after sunset – ships were not permitted to enter the harbour after sundown. There was also the daily firing of three shots during dum-dum, heralding the end of a day and the closing of the town gates.

Above: Fort Mirani is the second Portuguese fort built on this site, the first having been destroyed by a Turkish fleet while it was under construction. Left: Brass cannon guard the entrance to a Fort Mirani tower.

FORT JALALI

Fort Jalali, 'the glorious', was originally called Fort Joao. It was built by the Portuguese, who in 1527 were building for expediency, and they placed walls between existing towers. Together with Fort Mirani, Fort Jalali was to make Muscat a naval stronghold which helped the Portuguese to dominate and monopolise trade from the Red Sea to India. The fort in its present form was built by Melchoir Calcoa in 1588, as inscribed in a stone tablet in the fort's masonry, describing him as the founder and first captain.

Facing Fort Mirani across Muscat Bay, Fort Jalali is built on top of a rocky outcrop. The front of the fort is a long curtain wall with two tiers of embrasures and a round tower at each end. The only access is by a flight of steps cut into the rock on the harbour side. Early drawings of the fort show that the original construction consisted only of fortified spaces with boundaries of solid wall enclosing small garrison buildings on top of the mountain. The configuration of the fort has changed since that time, and Jalali now occupies the entire top of the rock on which it stands.

Events surrounding Fort Jalali coincided with those of Fort Mirani, from construction to battles, history, restoration and even skirmishes. A British resident reports in the early 1900s that, "At times the forts fall out, and they blaze away at each other across the harbour, and in front of the town, to the great interruption of business. We saw several marks on the face of Fort Jalali which testified to the occasional accuracy of the fire of Mirani."

Until the early 1970s Fort Jalali was used as a prison. Colonel David Smiley, who had commanded the Sultan's Armed Forces at Muscat, wrote in *Arabian Assignment* (1975) that one of his duties had been to visit the prisoners at Fort Jalali, "a veritable hellhole" housing about a hundred inmates herded indiscriminately together. However, Suzanne, Duchess of St. Albans, visited the fort a few years later, and wrote in her book *Where Time Stood Still*, that she had been "considerably surprised by the unexpectedly open and cheerful look of the place when I went to visit it. The whitewashed cells, which are different sizes, are above ground and equipped with ceiling fans, looking more like aviaries awaiting the next batch of exotic tropical birds than prison cells." Today Fort Jalali is a museum.

Left: The impregnable Fort Jalali was built by the Portuguese to protect the naval stronghold of Muscat.

SINGER

MUTRAH FORT

Mutrah Fort is a classic Arab fort, and a monument to Omani military architecture. Built by Omanis to their design, it is situated atop a mountain, where the Jebel Akhdar range meets the sea at Mutrah. Originally two towers were built by the Portuguese in the 16th century as part of Muscat's defence system. During the next century, the towers were strengthened by a curtain wall.

Eight watchtowers completed the fort's defences, each strategically located so that shelling from the fort could destroy any tower in the event of capture.

The fort fell twice to Turkish invasion, by admirals Piri Reis and Ali Beg, in the late 1500s. The capture of Mutrah Fort by the Omanis was a key point in ousting the Portuguese in 1654.

Restoration of Mutrah Fort began in 1979 and was completed in two years, using original construction methods which involved building walls by bonding boulders in lime or gypsum mortar.

Left: Sambouqs and boums lay anchor in Mutrah Harbour below the fort. Below: Fort Bait Al Falaj is so named because of the falaj which continues to run through it.

FORT BAIT AL FALAJ

The present Fort Bait Al Falaj in Ruwi was built in 1806 as Sultan Said bin Sultan's summer country house. It was also a fort, located in a strategic spot well protected by surrounding high mountains. Almost inaccessible, the fort controlled valleys which gave access to the coast of Muscat. Previous forts must have been located here, but the earliest recorded was destroyed in 1648 as part of a peace treaty between Imam Nasir bin Murshid and the Portuguese governor Dom Juliao de Naronha.

Saif bin Himyar attacked the Persians from his headquarters here in 1743. Saif's fort was probably restored by Seyyid Hamad bin Said bin Hamad, Regent of Muscat, when he moved the capital from Rustaq to Muscat in 1779.

Bait Al Falaj was the headquarters for Sultan Said and Captain Perronet Thompson's joint forces of 2,000 Omani troops and 402 British soldiers and Indian sepoys in 1820 when they were employed against the Wahhabi influenced Bani bu Ali tribe of the Ja'alan. Defeated in their first engagement because they underestimated the rigours of the Jebel Akhdar's natural defences, they attacked again successfully in 1821 under Sultan Said and Major General Lionel Smith.

The fort served as a stronghold of Sultan Faisal bin Turki from 1888 to 1913. From 1913 to 1918, Fort Bait Al Falaj was the Sultan's Armed Forces Headquarters. The last battle involving the fort was the Battle of Bait Al Falaj in 1915.

Sultan Qaboos decreed that the fort become the Armed Forces Museum, and after three years in restoration, the fort opened as a museum in 1988.

Photo: Ministry of Defence, Oman

SUR JAL

A good example of a small sur can be found at Jal along the Wadi Baushar near Muscat. It is a ruin, but the walls, towers and room divisions give a good idea of what a small sur was like. It is within a few hundred yards of the Fateh Castle Fort, which could have aided in its defence. Access to the towers of this sur is by climbing a rope to an opening in the upper wall.

The sur is an irregular rectangle with two round towers positioned at opposite diagonal corners. A machicolation is formed by an arch over the recessed gate near the southern tower. Entrance is through a guard room and a series of three doors. Construction is of mud bricks on stone footings.

SUR AL GHUBRAH

Sur Al Ghubrah is situated near Muscat. Only part of a tower of Sur Al Ghubrah still stands, the remainder of the building is a shallow mound of earth. This rectangular enclosure had two round towers of mud-brick walls on stone foundations located at diagonally opposite corners.

BAUSHAR CASTLE FORT

Baushar, now part of Muscat Municipality, is a small quiet village where the Batinah Plain meets the mountains. Baushar was once on the main camel route from Muscat to Nizwa and was also popular for its hot springs.

Among several castle forts and fortified residences in Baushar, the most impressive is the one believed to have been built by Mohammad Azzan Al Bu Said about 300 years ago. The last resident was Sheikh Hilal Ali Al Khalili in 1970. Today, although in ruins, the fort has retained a majestic aura.

FATEH CASTLE FORT

Fateh Castle Fort guarded a falaj and date palm grove in the Muscat area near Baushar, about four kilometres inland from the Gulf of Oman.

Although in a ruined state, enough remains of Fateh Castle Fort to show what a grand residence it once was. Not much is left of the fort wall, but the entrance to the castle contains a typical Omani carved door. Recessed within the remains of a pointed arch, this large door has four rows of bosses. The anf al-bab (the centre wood strip which overlaps the joint of the double doors) has a carved floral design, and carved geometrical designs cover the wide door frame.

WADI SAMAIL

Wadi Samail, also known as the Samail Gap, has long been the main trading and transport route from Muscat to the interior of Oman. Being a major thoroughfare, the Gap contains large numbers of military and castle forts, fortified towns and watchtowers to protect Omanis against centuries of attempted invasion.

Approaching the beginning of Samail Gap, travelling from Muscat to Izki, the first fortifications on today's hardtop highway are the towers of Rusayl and Al Jefnein. The old camel route would have taken the traveller past fortifications in Mutrah, Ruwi, Fateh, Baushar, Sunub and Rusayl, which is at the mouth of the Gap between Jebel Nakhl and Saih Hatat's towering mountains.

At Rusayl, a restored fortlet and watchtower are situated on a hill overlooking Wadi Samail. Access to the tower is through a 60 by 120-centimetre door, requiring a person to crawl into the tower. Within the tower, wooden rungs recessed into vertical slots in the wall permit access to the upper level. Standing at this level of the tower, one can imagine an Omani sentry, in the not-too-distant past, eyeing the countryside while lowering his long-barrel matchlock rifle into one of the down-sloping gun ports.

Across the wadi from Rusayl is Al Jefnein. The fort and tower have also been restored, only here the small fort has open walls, exposing the construction details and room layout of the interior.

Further along the wadi from Muscat to Izki, restored towers line the hilltops of Fanja, Bidbid, Al Hobe and Samail, and there is a very picturesque grouping of nine towers in Biaq. These silent sentinels bore witness to many hostilities and shared the defence of this vital route with the walled town of Fanja, and the forts at Bidbid, Samail, Al Hobe and Izki.

Many wadis cross the Gap, some cutting deep into Jebel Nakhl and Jebel Mahil to the west, others leading into the Eastern Hajar. At Bidbid, Wadi Aqq forks off towards the south-east and Sur.

Wadi Samail is so decidedly the major divide of the mountains that the areas on either side are named after their positions in relation to it – the Gharbiyah (Western Jebel) and the Sharqiyah (Eastern Jebel).

Above left: Watchtowers at Biaq are dwarfed by the imposing Jebel Akhdar. Above right: Towers abound on the porous rock at the village of Fanja.
Right: The fortlet and tower at Rusayl prior to their restoration in 1990.

FANJA

The old, brown-ochre walled town of Fanja rests against a massive multi-coloured mountainside above Wadi Samail. It is strategically located, controlling the passes between Muscat and the interior, and between the western and eastern mountains. From a distance the town appears deserted, but closer inspection reveals television antennae on a few mud-brick dwellings, and some newly restored houses. However, most of the inhabitants of Fanja have moved into the valley, in favour of access to homes with electricity and running water.

BIDBID FORT

Commanding a strategic position on the main route from Muscat to the interior, at the junction with the trade routes to Sur and Nizwa, Bidbid has always been an important town. The history of the fort, like that of many in Oman, is obscure. At the time it was built, it was possibly occupied by one of the local tribes, Bani Jabir, Siyabiyin or Rahbiyin.

The large, typical Omani design fort, is surrounded by the village of Bidbid and an extensive palm grove. Recessed in an Islamic-design pointed arch, the frame of the entrance door is decorated with a detailed floral pattern. Through this door forty-two steps lead up to the highest point of the fort – the two-storey watchtower. Probably built at different times, the fort has two separate courtyards with watchtowers. The gatehouse has a meeting room and four small windowless storerooms. The upper rooms were living quarters for the garrison. One room has a slit in the floor through which to hurl stones, shoot from, or pour hot honey on any enemies capable of crashing through the gateway. All the rooms have carved hardwood doors, and ceilings of palm trunk beams and reed matting supporting a layer of mud and gypsum. In the courtyard there is a 9- to 12-metre-deep well and a running falaj (irrigation channel).

Bidbid Fort was the first fort to be renovated in Oman after the decision was made to use only traditional techniques and materials in the repair of ancient forts. The walls were rendered with customary joos, a compound of fired mud, straw and gypsum. Saruj, a local cement mixture of baked lime and mud, was applied to the external walls. After fourteen months of painstaking work, the fort was restored to its former grandeur. Bidbid Fort has been used as the model for all subsequent fort renovations.

SAMAIL FORT

Samail is the name given to twelve connected, but unwalled villages which lie halfway along Wadi Samail. The sixteen kilometres of palm plantations, fields, watchtowers and large homes create a picturesque and luxuriant settlement. Samail is divided into two parts – Sufalat (Upper) Samail and Alayat (Lower) Samail.

At one time the upper and lower parts of the wadi were controlled by tribes hostile to each other. These enemy camps were divided by a small transverse ditch at Samail, called Shirkat Al Haida, across which many a fight took place among the constantly quarrelling and skirmishing tribes. In these moments of controversy, the combatants usually began by firing at each other across the Shirkat from a secluded spot, and then, passions rising with the intensity of the brawl, and infuriated by the taunts of their opponents, they would attack at close quarters with long double-edged Omani swords.

The main fort, in Upper Samail, stands on a precipitous cliff, the western side of this rocky eminence rising 90 metres above the wadi. It is an imposing structure, constructed by the builder of Rustaq Castle Fort, with a commanding position well-suited to its threefold purpose – to overawe the turbulent members of the community, to control the passageway of the Samail Gap, and to protect the whole settlement. The plan of the fort follows the rise and fall of the surrounding rock. The massive barbican is on the lowest side of the fort and contained the garrison captain's living quarters. The barbican is joined to a corner keep by low curtain walls of irregular shape and considerable length.

AL HOBE CASTLE FORT

Situated in the beautiful setting of the towering Jebel Akhdar, is the remote castle ruin of Al Hobe. Two kilometres off the Muscat to Izki road, through Wadi Samail, almost 80 kilometres from Nizwa, Al Hobe was at one time used as a residential retreat.

Although mostly in ruins, there remains some evidence that Al Hobe was once a splendid residence. The entrance door is asymmetrically divided with a finely carved anf al-bab (see Glossary). The door knockers are decorated with round metal plates. Within the main door are two small doors (wicket gates) with scalloped pointed arches. The door design is completed by the bosses, or bolt covers. Five watchtowers, on surrounding knolls, form a supplementary defence to the single tower of the fort.

IZKI FORT

Izki Fort was erected about 150 years ago on the site of a more ancient fort built by Mohammed Jabri, the maternal uncle of Seyyid Said bin Sultan. The British officer Colonel S.B. Miles visited Izki in 1876, and commented that, "Outside and in front of the castle, are two mounted iron guns, old, honeycombed and unsafe, but capable of making a prodigious noise, for they were fired as a salute on our arrival, and this is a quality of immeasurable value in a country where the use of artillery is so little known."

Izki Fort was evacuated in 1884 and surrendered to the Sultan under an agreement with the Bani Rowaiha tribe. The new Wali, Sheikh Mohammed, garrisoned the fort with Baluchis.

The fort lies next to the walled town of Izki, on an elevated site overlooking Wadi Halfain. It is a dilapidated but imposing fort ruin. Even today, in its greatly deteriorated state, one tower and a 1.5-metre-thick wall are impressive for their scale alone. The fort dominated the whole settlement, standing in its commanding position at the head of Samail Gap.

Izki lies at the furthest end of the Samail Gap from Muscat, and today it is a town of modern, colourful houses and shops. Before 1970, the residents lived in mud-brick houses, surrounded by high mud-brick walls which also enclosed and fortified the entire village. Izki was an important town in the early years of Oman history, and was the reputed home of the most reliable authority on early Oman history, Sirhan bin Sa'id bin Sirhan. His book, *Kashf al-ghummah* (*Dispeller of Grief*), was compiled in about 1728.

BIRKAT AL MAUZ CASTLE FORT

Birkat Al Mauz Castle Fort is another fine example of the combination of a fort and luxurious accommodation. It is located approximately 24 kilometres from Nizwa, at the beginning of Wadi Muaydin. The highest peaks of Jebel Akhdar provide a dramatic background to the fort's large mud-brick walls. The fort was built by Sultan bin Saif I, who also built Nizwa Fort. A superb falaj runs through the castle.

Lieutenant J.R. Wellsted mentioned the fort in 1835, when he wrote about Birkat Al Mauz (Banana Pool), "...it has a fort with a very spacious and good-looking castle, belonging to the Sheikh of Suwaiq, ...within its walls, around these are several large groves and plantations; the plantain trees are numerous and hence its name."

Birkat Al Mauz, along with Tanuf, was a focal point in the Jebel War of the 1950s. Suleiman bin Himyar, Sheikh of the powerful Bani Riyam tribe and known as 'Lord of the Green Mountain' had his family seat at Birkat Al Mauz. Jebel Akhdar was known as the Green Mountain not because of its colour, but because of its limestone, which is alive, or green, compared to dead lava. Suleiman joined forces with the newly elected Imam, Ghalib Al

Hina'i and his brother Talib bin Ali, in a rebellion against the Sultan in 1954.

In past struggles, if events took an adverse turn, rebels fighting in the area could retire to the strongholds of Birkat Al Mauz and Tanuf. If this failed, there was the impregnable retreat of Saiq at the top of Jebel Akhdar. As the Jebel War began to falter, the forces of Ghalib Al Hina'i and Talib bin Ali took refuge in these strongholds. Suleiman must have felt impregnably safe at his mountain top retreat in Saiq. However, a new element in warfare – airpower – had not been reckoned with. Assisted by the British Special Air Service (SAS), the Sultan's forces captured Birkat Al Mauz (which had only once before been taken by force – by the invading Persian army in 973 AD) and destroyed Tanuf and the fort at Saiq. With the destruction of their strongholds, the rebels capitulated.

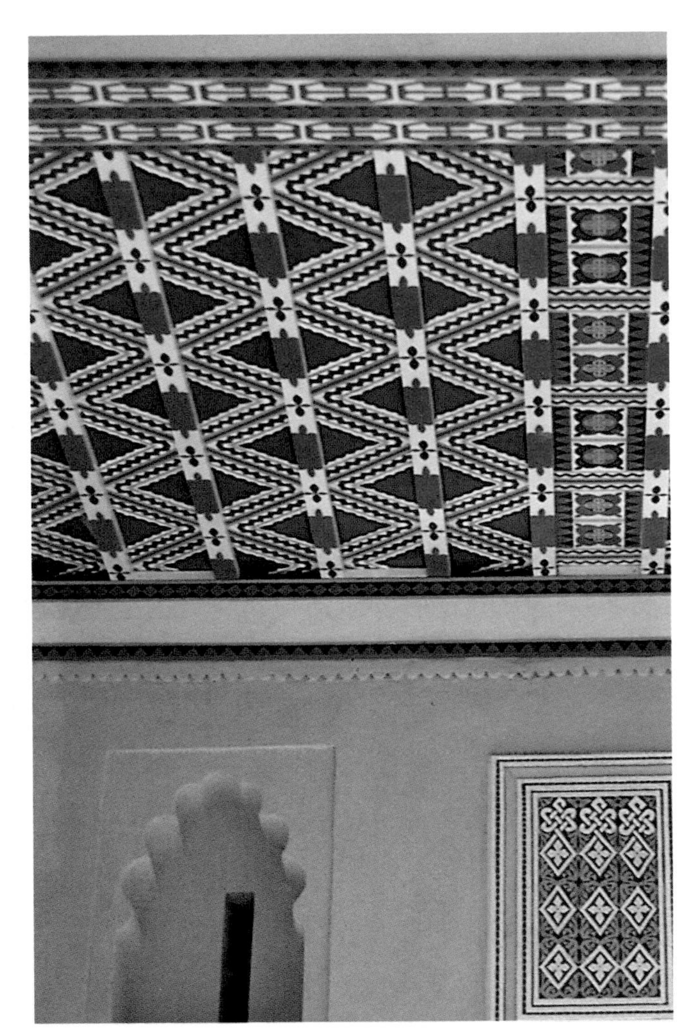

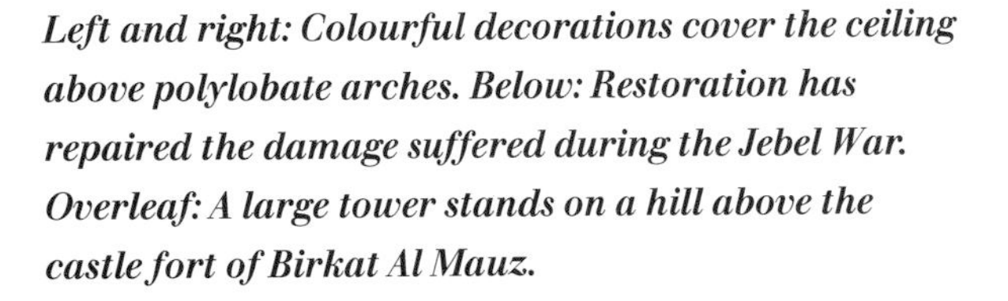

Left and right: Colourful decorations cover the ceiling above polylobate arches. Below: Restoration has repaired the damage suffered during the Jebel War. Overleaf: A large tower stands on a hill above the castle fort of Birkat Al Mauz.

MANAH

The old fortified town of Manah is approximately 11 kilometres south of Nizwa, and is believed to have been established during the invasion of the Sassanid king, Khusrau Anurshirwan, in the 6th century AD. However, there is no sign of great antiquity in the walled town. The mud and stone houses of Manah are similar in appearance to those throughout Oman. Manah is now abandoned, and in some areas its walls have crumbled. Only part of one square tower remains of two that were originally 51 metres high. Even now it is an impressive structure, built of unhewn stones and cement. Its red colour contrasts with surrounding tan mud houses. As Manah is situated on a flat plain, the high towers gave a commanding view, enabling guards to see any enemy approaching from a long distance.

FAIQAIN

Faiqain lies near Manah, south of Nizwa. It is a ghostly, abandoned, walled town, with a fort whose design differs from the conventional Omani design (see Introduction).

Faiqain Fort has massive walls and a windtower. Access to the fort is gained by climbing a rope up to an opening in the wall.

NIZWA

About 160 kilometres from Muscat, through the Samail Gap to the interior side of Jebel Akhdar, lies Nizwa. For a long time Nizwa was the spiritual heart of Oman and the centre of the defensive system of the interior. In the 18th century, Nizwa was referred to as 'holy Nizwa', and was the stronghold of the Imams. The earliest Imamate was established in 751 AD, when Al Julanda bin Masud, a member of the Azd tribe, became Imam. He remained the Imam until he was removed forcibly, and replaced by Mohammed bin Affan. Nizwa became the capital of the Imamate due to its central location. Rustaq was considered, but it would have been a more difficult area to defend.

It is believed that debris of forts dating back to the 12th century was used in the construction of the existing fort. This present structure was built by Sultan bin Saif I between 1670 and 1680, and represents the maximum expansion of the type of fort based on a gunnery tower.

It was built after the expulsion of the Portuguese from Oman, during the mid 17th century, and is of Omani design – the Portuguese had nothing to do with its origin or construction. Its purpose was to control the oasis and surrounding routes from Wadi Samail to the west, Wadi Tanuf to the east, and more remote desert regions to the south. Northern routes were defended by the mountains.

Approximately 36 metres in diameter, the fort rises to 30 metres, towering above the dwellings and souq clustered around it. The huge circular tower, known as the qila (citadel), stands at one corner of the hisn (large quadrangular enclosure). The circular tower is filled with earth to a level of 14 metres. The top of this solid-fill forms a horizontal circular platform with ports for cannon. This offered a 360° firing line above the surrounding palms. A massive wall rises above the platform for another 10.5 metres, and is topped by a circular walk, for musketeers to fire from behind crenellations. Entry is gained by a narrow zigzagging vaulted stairway through the solid-fill. At every turn there are doors which can be locked, to impede the progress of possible enemies. Further defence was probably by 'murder holes', through which any convenient projectile could be thrown down upon attackers.

Nizwa Fort appears impregnable to this day, solid and self-sufficient with its water supply from wells and a running falaj. Among the Omani, American and Spanish cannon lined around the parapet are several bearing the names of Imam Sultan bin Saif I and Kauli Khan – the Persian general who captured Muscat.

Left: Nizwa Fort, with its view of the modern mosque nearby, is guarded by a traditional askari. Below: The top of the fort's solid-fill forms a circular gun platform. Overleaf: Modern Omanis live and work in Nizwa's narrow lanes and beside her ancient fort.

Colonel Colin Maxwell describes the scene in Nizwa after the Jebel War: "... on 24 December, 1955, the Sultan triumphantly arrived in Nizwa amid shattering explosions from the fort's cannon, filling the sky with blue smoke and disintegrating some of the looser bits of the battlements. With cannon firing, spasmodic rifle fire, shouting citizens, roaring trucks, something approaching pandemonium ruled in Nizwa that morning."

Wendel Phillips, an American archaeologist, described his 1958 visit to Nizwa Fort: "We were led past crowds of people standing outside the fort, through a large outer gate and a smaller inner gate, then up two flights of stairs to the majlis or Imam's audience chamber.

When our eyes became adjusted to the dim light of the interior, we saw a thin old man wearing a large white turban on his head and sitting on a rug at the further end of a rather long room. On his right were a couple of old men similarly attired and on either side of him were seated his bodyguard of armed men.... he asked Mr Dykstra to sit on his right and me on his left. The coffee and halwah (sweetmeats) were next passed and then the rose water was sprinkled over us."

Near Nizwa Fort there is a stone watchtower surrounded by shops. Another tower, which was part of the wall around the old city, is located near the souq. Along the road entering Nizwa from Bahla, is an unusual round tower with a long thin tower attached to one side.

Only a few remnants of the old Nizwa wall remain today but tall mud houses line narrow dusty streets as they have for centuries. Most of these buildings are fortified structures, to protect the occupants against their neighbours. When Ibn Batuta, a writer living in the late 13th and early 14th centuries, visited Nizwa in 1329, he commented on the beautiful bazaars. The bazaar, or souq, is still popular today, drawing visitors from as far away as Muscat and beyond. A huge ancient tree provided shade for the animal auctions for many years, but the animal auctions have now moved to the western side of Nizwa.

A current 'beautification project' is changing the face of Nizwa. Restoration of the fort, including the removal of shops from its base, has returned the fort to its former grandeur.

Left: The fardha, which gives access to the falaj, continues to be used in Tanuf today. Right and below: The ruins of Tanuf are a sombre reminder of the Jebel War.

TANUF

Tanuf lies along Wadi Tanuf at the mouth of a cavernous gorge in the giant mountains of Jebel Akhdar. The walled town was the stronghold of Suleiman bin Himyar (see page 42) in the 1950s. Before him, Himyar bin Nasir and the Sheikhs of the Bani Riyam were 'Lords of the Green Mountain'.

In the past, if the Bani Riyam positions in Tanuf or Birkat Al Mauz were untenable during a period of danger, the Bani Riyam would retreat to the unapproachable dark limestone cliffs and remain impregnably lodged. In the 1950s, Suleiman played an important part in the Jebel War. For this the Sultan requested the RAF to attack Tanuf, Birkat Al Mauz and the mountain-top haven, Saiq.

In 1900, a visitor to Tanuf wrote, "At noon on the third day of my stay here, set out for the Green Mountains, and two hours' ride brought me to the small town of Tanoof, distant six or seven miles from Nuswee. This is a pretty little place, surrounded by a wall pierced with loopholes and two small gates. A castle stands at the eastern extreme with a fine flourishing date grove to the westward. The houses built of mud and stone, are small, and the population about three hundred."

Parts of buildings, walls and mounds of earth where mud bricks have disintegrated, are all that remain of Tanuf. Tanuf is like a memorial to the ancient way of life in Oman.

BAHLA

There is an aura of history about Bahla. Wadi Bahla is one of the areas in the Gulf where evidence of important human occupation, between the third and first millennia BC, has been discovered. The handsome fort is called Hisn Tamah after the Nebhani chief of that name who is thought to have built it over the ruin of an ancient, perhaps Parthian, structure.

The fort stands on an enormous sandstone outcrop dominating a plain. It is a large, sturdy structure, once very beautiful. A unique feature was its two windtowers, probably the tallest edifices in Oman. They are shown still intact in an 1885 photo by the British Colonel, S.B. Miles, but unfortunately little remains of these towers today. The extent of present ruins reflect the status of the fort, and perhaps current renovations will restore Bahla Fort to its former grandeur. Being the site of many conflicts, the fort has probably experienced many restorations throughout the years. Bahla is noted in UNESCO's World Heritage list as a monument of global importance.

The grandiose fort provided the major defence for the walled town of Bahla. From the fort the mud-brick wall, which is said to have been designed and built by a woman named Gheitha about 600 years ago, twists around surrounding hills for a distance of 13 kilometres. Defensive turrets, which are towers built into the wall, occur at frequent intervals. Here sentries kept a sharp lookout for unfriendly neighbours or marauding desert tribes. The surrounding stark bare rock mountains stand in dramatic contrast to the cultivated land and date palms within the wall.

Bahla ranks as one of the finest walled cities in the world. At one time it was noted for its witchcraft. Today the predominant craft is pottery.

JABRIN CASTLE

This castle fort stands in the middle of a small oasis, its mass rising above a grove of palms about 20 kilometres from Bahla. Also called the Palace of Imam Bil'arub bin Sultan, it is the most handsome fort in Oman. Unique in sheer scale, it was grandiose, forbidding and a symbol of ascendancy. Built by Bil'arub bin Sultan around 1675 over the remains of a previous structure, it became a prototype in Oman for huge defensive castles constructed of stones bound with mortar. Bil'arub moved the capital of Oman from Nizwa to Jabrin when he became Imam in 1688.

The fort is a multi-storey building complex of overlapping and interlocking structures, with two adjacent courtyards. The buildings are divided by different floor levels and joined by a narrow corridor on the upper section of the castle.

Jabrin is one of the finest examples of Omani fort architecture. Its latticed and stone-mullioned windows look out over a flat plain and the sharp outline of Jebel Akhdar. Turrets and trellised balconies give the appearance of a Renaissance palace. Islamic and floral designs are painted on wooden ceiling beams in the Hall of the Sun and Moon, and in several other rooms. Plastered walls have high arched recesses, some around windows, that diffuse light and aid in ventilation.

The palace is situated in the northern area of a fortified courtyard. A large tamarind tree near the entrance has provided shade for man and beast for many years. (The British Colonel, S.B. Miles, recorded that he camped nearby in 1885.) At diagonally opposite corners of the building are two great jutting towers with walls two metres thick. They provided a wide firing range, defending all four sides of the fortified palace from attack. The southwest corner tower contains two gun-battery levels. A machicolation over the palace gate provided a protected platform from which to drop stones or hot oil on enemies approaching the main entrance.

Vaulted niches curving to an arch at the top, fine decorated plaster, delicate colours, the blending of light and shade, make each room a work of art. The plasterwork of some passageway arches is delicately patterned with Koranic inscriptions and geometrical designs in black and red. Polylobate arches provide entrances to rooms around the courtyard. Another feature of the fort was the madrassa, or religious college, established by Imam Bil'arub bin Sultan. He also had a second-floor room for his favourite horse.

The innermost recesses of the fort contain four dungeons, each of them displaying different degrees of unpleasantness. The meeting room has hidden corners for guards, and a false floor. A secret escape route tunnels deep into the fort.

Bil'arub bin Sultan died at Jabrin in 1692, after a siege by his brother Saif bin Sultan I. His tomb is in the fort. Saif removed the capital to Rustaq, but a few years after his death in 1711, the capital returned to Jabrin under Imam Mohammed bin Nasir. He made Jabrin his headquarters during the civil war of 1722-24. After his death in 1728, Jabrin Castle Fort remained dormant until restoration in 1983.

Right: The forbidding exterior of Jabrin Castle Fort conceals an embellished palace complex.
Overleaf: Detail from one of the principal rooms illustrates a fine example of Omani ceiling-painting.

SULAIF

On a high bank of the Wadi Al Ain where it meets with Wadi Sunaisal, the remains of the fortified city of Sulaif blend in colour and texture with the jebel outcrop. Old Sulaif and its fort have long been abandoned for the village of air-conditioned cement block houses outside the walls. Many residents went to Ibri, a distance of about 11 kilometres, which is visible from the towers on Sulaif's walls.

Many stone tablets in the old walled town are inscribed with poems and messages.

DHAHIRAH REGION

The Dhahirah lies between Nizwa and Buraimi. Situated on the southern flanks of the Western Hajar, this area is rich in archeological sites. Grave mounds discovered near Dank date from the early 3rd millennium BC.

On his last journey through the interior of Oman, in 1885, Colonel S.B. Miles was keen to visit the Dhahirah: "I gazed upon the little-known, wild plain of Al Dhahirah, the desert province of Oman."

The watchtowers, found in and around the villages and wadis of the Dhahirah, saw much action during the late 19th century when the region went through numerous transferences of power from one faction to another. There are interesting towers at Araqi (left), Subaikhi and Yankal.

IBRI

The city of Ibri today extends beyond the confines of the old walled city (above and left). Modern brightly coloured buildings spaced along paved streets reflect the new attitudes of its inhabitants, unlike a few years ago.

Ibri is one of the oldest inhabited areas in Oman. Evidence has been unearthed disclosing a pre-historic population. Through the centuries it was a remote area, remaining until very recently an old-fashioned city untouched by tourism.

Outsiders were not welcome in Ibri, as the British officers, Lieutenant J.R. Wellsted and Lieutenant F. Whitelock discovered during their visit to Ibri in 1836, which happened to be at the same time as the Wahhabis were on a warring march towards Oman. Wellsted and Whitelock made a hasty retreat from the city, narrowly escaping serious injury when pelted with stones. Wellsted noted, "The neighbouring Arabs observe that to enter Ibri a man must either go armed to the teeth or as a beggar with a cloth, and not of decent quality, round his waist." He also commented that outlaws from the surrounding desert area brought their loot to sell at the 'thieves market', the largest and busiest bazaar in the Dhahirah Region.

Major General Cox wrote on a later visit to Ibri, "... on the march to Ibri we were fired on from a distant encampment, and bullets whizzed across our bows, but I was now used to this little amenity, which appeared to be ordinary practice of a Badawi community – based on the strange assumption that any mounted party seen approaching must be enemies on a raid. Apparently the etiquette is to stop and return the fire if you really are an enemy, otherwise ride on and take no notice."

MUSCAT CITY

"Muscat Bay is, to my mind, the most wonderful that nature and art could ever devise. It is surrounded in a deep semicircle by high precipitous rocks, which the Portuguese have topped with watchtowers." So stated the German traveller Englebert Kaempfer in 1688 AD. The appearance of the coast from the sea is indeed extremely attractive, but the rugged dark hills rising one range above another, until apparently joining the great backrange which rises to 1,800 metres, have been much more to the city than a picturesque backdrop. They have afforded it excellent natural defences which the Portuguese supplemented with forts, walls and watchtowers.

Before 1929 travellers could get to Muscat only by boat or by donkey, and prior to 1972 the three main gates of Muscat's city wall – Bal Al Kabir, Bab As Saghir and Bab Al Matha'ib – were closed at sunset, in time for the ceremony of dum-dum. Dum-dum was marked by the firing of a cannon from Fort Mirani. No one was permitted to enter or leave the city until the gates opened after sunrise.

In his diary, Englebert Kaempfer commented on the male residents of Muscat: "Men dress in a long wide coat of linen with wide sleeves and a belt around the waist. On this they wear a wide unlined coat. Their sandals have leather thongs. They wrap their head in long white towels, with their ends hanging down from their head or shoulder; and their khanjar or dagger is worn by the side."

Lieutenant William Heude, a British officer, visited Muscat in 1816, and in his book, *A Voyage up the Persian Gulf*, observed: "The custom-house, the palace, and its vicinity, the bazaars and the principal streets, were

crowded with Arabs of every description and tribe; with Hindoos, Beloochies, Tirks, and Africans. The Arabs, each after the manner of his tribe, or his own convenience, with a curved asgailee, a matchlock, or a pike; the Beloochie soldiers, naked to the waist, with a crooked toffung, a knife, and a straight two-handed sword; the wild Bedooin might be distinguished from amongst the first, by a striped kerchief surrounded with lashes of whipcord, and flying loosely around his head..."

Muscat came under Portuguese domination in 1507 after the fall of Kalhat, Sur and Quriyat. In 1581 the Turkish admiral Ali Beg took Muscat after a month's seige, but made no attempt to hold it permanently. The Portuguese returned and strengthened their position by completing Fort Mirani. The Portuguese were routed from Muscat in 1650, by Sultan bin Saif I. However, the recovery of the well-defended Muscat was made easier by a Gujerati trader named Narrotum. Narrotum, a man of wealth and influence in Muscat, had a beautiful daughter with whom the Portuguese governor of Muscat, Pereira, fell in love. When his excellency demanded her hand in marriage, Narrotum was horrified at the idea of his child marrying a Christian. But fearing the vengeance of a love-sick governor if he refused permission, he feigned compliance, and asked for a year's time in which to prepare the bride's trousseau upon a scale befitting the governor. Pereira granted the delay.

In the meantime the city was under siege by Sultan bin Saif I, who could make little progress against the excellent defences of Muscat. Narrotum then contrived a scheme to thwart the marriage and at the same time deliver the fortifications to Sultan bin Saif I. He presented wedding plans to the governor which included dressing up Fort Mirani. He said that water in the fort's tanks was bad and should be renewed, and that the grain was infested with bugs and should be replaced with good grain. The gunpowder too, he said, was old and unreliable. Why not fill the magazines with fresh gunpowder? Pereira agreed, authorising Narrotum to replenish the stores. Once the water tanks were empty for cleaning, and the grain and gunpowder had been removed to make room for the new, Narrotum sent word to Sultan bin Saif I to attack the city. The Imam attacked and passed the city wall without difficulty. The two forts, Mirani and Jalali, were taken by escalade. The guns would not go off, for the powder had been tampered with and the garrison could make no effective resistance.

Before 1972 old Muscat was crowded with mud-brick buildings, crumbling walls, rubble, flaking plaster, padlocked wooden doorways, rickety staircases, barred windows and dusty paths. Muscat today reflects Oman's step forward into the 20th century whilst maintaining its ties with the past. The two forts, Mirani and Jalali, remind us of the sometimes turbulent past, while the modern palace has replaced the old residence of past sultans. New government buildings using traditional Islamic design features have taken the place of the mudbrick dwellings, and although sections of the city wall have been renovated with traditional mud-brick construction, on the whole the wall and gates have a contemporary appearance.

The city gates now stand open, and instead of being defensive and inward-looking, the city is the hub of routes leading outwards through the Samail Gap to the interior, along the Batinah Coast towards Musandam, and south to Salalah.

AL KHAWD

Inland, about 13 kilometres from Seeb on the Batinah Plain, are a majestic castle fort and the remains of a military fort. The ruins of the old military fort – two watchtowers and part of a stone and mud-mortar wall – straddle the top of a rocky outcrop overlooking Wadi Al Khawd on one side and the old village of Al Khawd on the other. The top of the Al Khawd Castle Fort rises in the distance, above an extensive palm plantation.

The castle fort was built by Hmeyyid bin Ameid bin Ali Al Hinai about 1865. His descendants lived in the fort continuously until 1979, when his 90-year-old great grandson, Mohammed bin Ameid bin Hmeyyid moved into contemporary structures built next to the castle fort. Every Friday male members of the family meet in the majlis of the new buildings, continuing the local tradition of exchanging stories and news, eating dates and halwa (sweetmeats), and drinking cardamom-flavoured qahwa (Omani coffee). The front of the castle is very decorative, with windows of east African influence and a richly carved door imported from Zanzibar. A round tower is located at one corner of the building facing the distant ruins of the military fort, and a lone rusting cannon juts out from a gun port in the castle wall.

Details from Al Khawd Castle Fort create an elegant contrast to the ruins of the military fort (opposite).

SUR RUMAIS

A moat surrounds Sur Rumais, and remains of the original sur indicate that there may have been a defended bridge across the trench. The walls of this square sur are built of rectangular mud bricks faced in stone. At the corners are round towers – two made of limestone and the other two of mud bricks with stone facing. The sur had a triple-arched entryway. A sentry-walk, formed by cantilevered stone slabs, spans the main wall. Stone stairways give access to three of the four towers, and carved, stylised floral motifs decorate the lintel of a wooden door.

The remains of a mosque stand a few metres from the moat. Most of the Batinah aswar had a mosque which was located outside the compound, but always nearby.

SUR AL UQDAH

The remains of this sur, located near Barka, indicate that the rectangular enclosure was surrounded by either a secondary wall or a moat. The fortified gate has a 90° angled entry under a three-storey square tower.

Left and opposite: Stone construction has preserved Sur Rumais. Above and below: The outer fortifications of Sur Al Uqdah have collapsed.

BARKA FORT

Only a few hundred metres from the shore of the Gulf of Oman, in the centre of the historic town of Barka, is Barka Fort. Restored in 1986, its great height makes it very conspicuous from the sea. At the rear of the fort are two restored watchtowers, which were once part of Barka's town wall.

In the 18th century Barka was one of the most important towns on the Batinah Coast. The Persians occupied Barka until the mid-18th century. Around 1744 when the Persians reduced their forces, Imam Ahmed bin Said forced the remaining garrisons to come to terms. In 1747 the last contingent of the Persian garrison in Barka was invited to a banquet. By a pre-arranged signal, many of the Persians were slaughtered. Survivors were put in a boat which was then put to sea and set afire. Thus ended the Persian presence in Oman. In 1781, Barka was a centre of tribal conflict.

Barka Fort is constructed mainly of stone rather than mud bricks. One of the four large towers is an unusual octagonal shape. A few cannons are at gun ports in the towers. Lieutenent J.R. Wellsted, who visited the fort in 1836, reported thirty pieces of artillery. His visit was restricted to one tower as the Seyyid's harem was quartered in the fort.

The most interesting room in the fort is the Imam's reception hall. Oriental carpets cover the floor from wall to wall, and pillows line the walls. The appearance is not that of a museum, but of a room alive, ready to receive guests. Today the Wali of Barka receives local officials and guests in this majlis every Monday.

MUSLIMAT

About 300 years ago the walled village of Hugarah, now part of Muslimat, was established along Wadi Al Mawil. Hugarah's defensive structure was a giant watchtower erected in the centre of the compound (below), in contrast to the usual practice of placing towers at the corners of the town walls. Nakhl Fort is in clear view from this tower.

About 1890, Mohammed Salem Mohammed Al Rawahi built an elaborate mansion along the wall near the village entrance. His son added a second level thirty years later. Sheikh Saif Abdullah Aziz Mohammed Salem Rawahi resided here until 1984 when he moved into a new modern house nearby. His son, who lives in an adjacent house, is Wali of Sohar, Buraimi, Kabourah, Quriyat, Shinas, Yankal and Suwaiq.

Most of the mud-brick houses within the walled town are in good condition and the one-storey mud-brick mosque is still in use today. Its interior has round columns topped with arches. Around the mihrab (left), is a beautiful wall decorated with three-dimensional designs in plaster. Inside the main gate, Bab Sabah Al Hugarah, a stone stairway leads to the mosque and a second-storey room where parts of ropes hang from the beam where water was once drawn from a deep well.

Hugarah experienced a few hostile periods. One of these periods was during the Portuguese expulsion in 1650. Another time was around 1920 when a conflict flared over the Imam of Nakhl's unsuccessful attempt to include the territory of Hugarah as part of Nakhl.

NAKHL FORT

The town of Nakhl lies in a secluded glen below the lofty mass of Jebel Nakhl, which rises to a height of 1588 metres. It is a quiet village until its peace and tranquillity are shattered on weekends and holidays by Omanis who come by car and bus to picnic in cool shady areas along the wadi. Hot springs flow from the mountain rocks, forming a continuous running stream, a not-too-frequent sight and sound in Oman.

Standing within a gorge and protected by the mountains around it, Nakhl Fort was considered invulnerable by the Omanis who had a deep sense of its military strength. Owing to its position, the fort has played an important part in the history of Oman during the past three centuries, particularly in the final years of the Ya'ruba Dynasty.

About 1769 Nakhl Fort was besieged by Imam Mohammed bin Sultan with men recruited from the Sharqiyah Region. The fort suffered severe damage from cannon fire, but was saved by reinforcements from the Al Zahira tribe.

The fort, restored in 1990, stands on an eminence overlooking the town and Wadi Nakhl. Access is by a steep ramp leading up to the main gateway and through a strong outer rampart. Loopholes, or openings in the wall flaring outwards, permit the firing of a battery of iron cannon. A keep, the most secure part of the fort, stands in the courtyard, and consists of a high curtain wall flanked by two towers. From the towers' battlements, there is a superb view of the Batinah Plain.

As well as Fort Nakhl being a major tourist attraction, the majlis (above centre) serves as a weekly meeting place for the Wali of Nakhl.

WADI AWABI

Wadi Awabi was controlled by a stone fort (right) which now has a renovated tower at one corner and a non-renovated, but well-preserved, tower at the diagonally opposite corner. Two old cannons are partially buried in the rocky land. The dark grey mountains here are limestone, rich in fossils, and are as much as 250 million years old. Along this scenic wadi, a partial tower in Sital (left) keeps company with a lone tree. At the village of Mahsanah (above), which rises high above the wadi, a substantial tower is predominant among the houses. The residences are colourful and of a design reminiscent of Yemeni architecture.

RUSTAQ CASTLE

Just beyond the Batinah Plain between low-lying red mountains and the massive Jebel Akhdar, is the oasis village of Rustaq with its dominating castle fort. It was called Qalat Al Kisra, after the Persian who controlled the land between Sohar and Rustaq in the 7th century. The Persian military governor, Wahraz, built a castle in Rustaq in about 600 AD.

As political control passed from one tribe to another and from one city to another, unoccupied forts deteriorated, accounting for the continuous rebuilding of forts through the centuries. The rebuilt fort was usually larger than the previous, with new sections added. This was the case with Rustaq.

The Julandas built Rustaq Castle Fort on the Persian ruins in 1250 AD. When Nasir bin Murshid became the first Ya'ruba ruler in 1624, he moved the capital from Bahla to Rustaq and rebuilt the fort there in 1650. This is the fort standing today, although one tower was added in 1744 by Imam Ahmed bin Said, and another in 1906 during the reign of Sultan Faisal bin Turki.

Rustaq has been through several tumultuous and politically influential periods, right up to the 1950s when, as Talib bin Ali's home, it featured prominently in the Jebel War. Colonel Colin Maxwell described the action:

"The Sultan's Batinah Force had just mounted a dawn attack from Hazm and captured the qarn (small hill) astride the approach from the coast to Rustaq. Talib bin Ali and his askaris (East African native soldiers or policemen) were preparing to counter-attack our positions dominating the qarn, and Talib's three-ton truck had been observed ferrying reserves up to within small-arms range of our positions. As the truck approached for the third time that afternoon, I ordered my Bren gunners to open fire. The vehicle was caught in a withering cross-fire and came to an abrupt halt as its occupants leapt off it and went to ground.

Unknown to us at the time but told to me afterwards by an askari passenger, Talib himself was in the vehicle; our bullets had ripped through the soft-skinned vehicle and wounded four of Talib's askaris, missing Talib by inches; leaping from the truck he had taken cover in a disused well where he remained for several hours until returning to Rustaq under cover of darkness."

***Right:** The dominating castle fort at Rustaq.*
***Overleaf:** Tabaqa Fort, with its defence tower clinging to the cliff, keeps watch over Wadi Sahtan, near Rustaq.*

AL HAZM FORT

Sultan bin Saif II, who became Imam in 1711, had built the great angular fort at Al Hazm in 1708 with finances from various seafaring activities. Located where the Batinah Plain meets Jebel Akhdar, it lies in a date palm grove surrounded by the village. Sultan bin Saif II moved the capital from Rustaq to Al Hazm in 1711.

Al Hazm Fort is a true military fort, incorporating towers for many cannons, and loopholes in the upper floor for musketeers to fire through. Hazm became a model for subsequent defensive structures. Its massive wooden entry door is strong enough to repel any invaders.

A small entry door permits one person, crouching, to enter an inclined passageway to a second massive wooden door. Inside is a maze of corridors and small rooms, a round room for storing dates, another for rice, a madrassah (Koranic school), a kitchen, and living quarters for the Imam and his wives. A fast-flowing freshwater falaj runs through the fort. There is a large enclosure for storing water in the event of the falaj being cut off by an enemy. Another room was for boiling honey or oil which was then poured from the machicolation extending over the entrance onto invaders able to penetrate that far.

The central support columns, which blend into domed ceilings in the two towers, are profusely decorated. Portuguese and Omani cannons point through gun ports towards the countryside and the fort's outer walls. Doorways and passages are lavishly decorated with carved stone and plaster mouldings, deserving of a royal residence. Yet there is an economy of space. Gun ports in walls cover every inner court. A flight of stairs is inclined at an angle to permit the riding of a horse stabled in an upper level room. There were two escape tunnels, one of which went all the way to the fort at Rustaq, a distance of 32 kilometres. Three dungeons complete the medieval atmosphere of Al Hazm Fort. One dungeon was for short-term prisoners, a second for long terms and the third for life, which under the harsh conditions was not usually very long.

Sultan bin Saif II died here in 1718 and was buried in a walled-up tomb in the fort. When he was succeeded by 12-year-old Saif bin Sultan II, dissenters began a 12-year civil war.

***Left:** Details of the interior of Al Hazm show the intricate wood and stone carvings, and an upper level opening which increases ventilation and light below. **Right:** The exterior of the fort and falaj.*

SUR AL MULADDAH

It has now been concluded through research that Sur Al Muladdah (above), once considered to have been surrounded by a moat, in fact had an external, lesser wall. This lesser wall is believed to have had corner towers on the southern side, but has now been reduced to rubble. Surviving is the large mud-brick sur with walls containing a sentry-walk, and part of a three-storey entrance. The once three-storey towers of round stones and saruj plaster have survived only up to the second storey.

SUR AL QARAT

Two round towers and an attractive and substantial gate-house are all that remain of this sur in Al Qarat (right). It was a large mud-brick enclosure with three-storey towers built of stone and saruj.

The towers have a solid-walled first storey, gun ports at the upper levels, and are topped with crenellated parapets. The three-storey gate-house is built of stone, which accounts for its good condition, the mud-brick walls having long been a mound of debris. The third storey of the gate-house is defended by a parapet with arrow-slits and crenellations, and the entrance is crowned by an ogee arch. A machicolation (kuwwa) defends the entry-gate where the door lintel is recessed, leaving a space between the upper floor and the outer wall.

BAIT NA'MAN CASTLE FORT

The 17th-century residence at Bait Na'man has the character of a rich country house, and was constructed by Imam Saif bin Sultan I (died 1711 AD) for his exclusive use. Situated in a large palm grove which extends for several kilometres west of Muscat, the castle is an imposing structure which contrasts with the barasti shelters of the villagers. The earliest written reference to Bait Na'man, refers to Imam Saif bin Sultan, who planted 30,000 young date palm trees and 6,000 coconut trees. Water for the plantation was supplied by falaj (irrigation channels) and zajarah (animal-powered wells). The building of Bait Na'man is among the many achievements of the political and economic renaissance which took place in Oman under the Ya'ruba Imams (1624–1741). During their reign, Al Hamra in Jebel Akhdar, and Birkat Al Mauz were created. They also revived interest in Ibra, Quriyat, Barka, Jabrin and Al Hazm.

Besides its main function of a country house, Bait Na'man was used as a rest-house by Imam Ahmed bin Said (1741-1775) who would stay there for several days on his way between Muscat and Rustaq. During these stops he would give audience to the people of the area from Masna'ah to Seeb. Two of his sons used Bait Na'man as a residence for several years.

The most important historical event related to Bait Na'man is the fight between Said bin Sultan (1804-1856), and the Regent of Muscat, Badr bin Saif. Badr was a staunch supporter of the Wahhabis, and had developed an expansionist policy towards Oman. Badr planned to murder Said, but Said decided to dispatch the plotter at a meeting in Bait Na'man. The story goes that the two men met inside the building and fought with daggers. Badr was wounded in the fight, escaped through a window and fled on horseback. He eventually fell from his horse and was soon overtaken and finished off by Said bin Sultan and his men. A party of Wahhabi horsemen found Badr dead and proceeded to the castle. However, they were scared away by Said's followers, who were pointing rifles at them from the crenellations atop Bait Na'man's walls. This episode marked the beginning of the long reign of Said bin Sultan and one of the most prosperous periods in the history of Oman.

Mentioned mostly as a meeting place for parties of armed men or as a stopover for distinguished travellers, Bait Na'man continued to be used until a few decades ago.

Left top: During restoration in 1990, this section of original ceiling was left intact. Left below: The walled courtyard assured privacy. This page top: Unusual domes topped Bait Na'man's towers. This page below: Light filters through one of the castle's restored windows.

The remains of Sur Al Billah (top left) and Sur Bu Abali.

SUR AL BILLAH

A few kilometres from Bait Na'man are the ruins of a small square mud-brick enclosure with a stone and saruj fortified entrance. Two large round towers are built at diagonal corners. The base of one tower remains while the mud bricks of the opposite corner tower have disintegrated into a mound of earth. Smooth straight paths outline the location of former walls.

SUR BU ABALI

The sur at Bu Abali, near Barka, is square. It is made of mud-brick and, similar to many sur in the area, has two round towers placed at diagonal corners. A stone and saruj fortified entrance leads into a 90° angled passageway containing two doors in a three-storey tower.

SUR THARMAD

Splendidly restored, Sur Tharmad is west of Barka along the dual highway from Muscat to Sohar. The fortress is a variation on the traditional square sur, which normally had round towers at all four corners. Only three of the Sur Tharmad corner towers are round. The round NW tower is joined to the walls by a salient section lower than the tower. The fourth tower, positioned on the south wall, slightly in from the SW corner, is a large rectangle.

The tall barbican, recessed within the northern wall of the sur, has a beautiful rich mahogany entrance door built within an off-centre pointed arch. Inside the sur are the remains of rooms built against the exterior walls.

SUR MIRABSHAH

This restored sur, near Suwaiq, is a mud-brick enclosure defended by four three-storey round towers located at the corners. The entrance is through a pointed arched doorway in a three-storey square tower. At the second level of the towers there are small square gun ports and a few loopholes. At the third level are platforms defended by crenellated parapets with small arrow slits.

SUWAIQ FORT

West of Barka, on the Gulf of Oman, is the quiet fishing village of Suwaiq. In the 18th century, the village had an active port equal to Barka, Masna'ah and Sohar.

From time to time the flow of life in the village and fort has been interrupted by violent events. During the reign of Said bin Sultan, in circa 1830, Seyyid Qais bin Azzan Al Bu Said of Rustaq formed a plot to destroy him and seize the government of Muscat. He shared his plan with his cousin, Seyyid Hilal bin Mohammed Al Bu Said, Wali of Suwaiq, seeking approval and support for this venture. Seyyid Hilal indignantly denounced the plot. Seyyid Qais was then determined to seek revenge on his cousin. Failing to find an assassin, he undertook the task himself. In a friendly manner he approached Hilal, who, unlike most men of his rank, seldom wore a sword. Qais suddenly drew his sword and struck Hilal savagely on the head. Staggered by the unexpected blow, Hilal recovered sufficiently to plunge his dagger into his assailant.

Around 1836, Suwaiq Fort was attacked while it was being defended by Seyyid Hilal's wife, who was well-known for her valour. While Hilal was under safe conduct in Muscat, a force sent by the Imam arrived in Suwaiq with the purpose of seizing the fort. Threats were made that if the fort did not surrender, her husband would be put to death. She is said to have scorned the attackers, calling their bluff and responding: "Go back to those who sent you, and tell them that I shall defend the fort to the utmost of my power; and if they choose to cut him to pieces before me, they will find no alteration in my resolution." The enemy retreated.

Lieutenant J.R. Wellsted, the first of two Europeans to penetrate the interior of Oman, in writing of this event noted, "Hilal feels the greatest respect for, and stands in some awe of this dame, without whose advice and concurrence he undertakes nothing of moment."

The architecture of Suwaiq Fort is different from that of the traditional Omani fort (see Introduction). Suwaiq Fort sports round towers at three corners, and a square tower (pre-cannon architecture) at the other corner. The square keep contrasts with the round towers.

SUR AL BU HILAL

Located within sight of Sur Mirabshah, this enclosure (right) covers an area equal to a small town. It is a vast mud-brick sur defended by three round towers and a rectangular protuberance. One of the round towers has an unusually shaped turret.

Within the compound was a small fortlet with two towers. Near it stood a single isolated tower. This sur was recently renovated except for the interior, where only the remains of the inner fort's narrow rooms still stand.

SUR AL BU RASHID

Sur Al Bu Rashid (left) is located in Al Khadra. It is a large square mud-brick enclosure probably built to enlarge a smaller sur. Two large towers are at the NW and SE corners, with a third tower located mid-way along the west wall. The fourth tower is at the entrance and appears to form a defence for a smaller compound contained within the sur. Close to the sur are five small mosques which form an arc pattern.

SUR QASABIYAT AL BU SAID

Near Al Khaburah are the imposing remains of a large sur. Rectangular, with round towers at three corners, the enclosure has two curved walls at the west corner which give the impression of forming part of a fourth round tower but are, in fact, the remnants of an unusual room. A fortified entrance in a two-storey building on the NE wall is partly restored. One three-storey tower is well preserved. The first storey has a solid outer wall made from bands of wadi-bed stones laid in a herring-bone pattern. Gun ports are around the second storey, while the third storey has a crenellated parapet.

WADI HAWASINAH

From Al Khaburah on the Gulf Coast, Wadi Hawasinah leads through the Hajar Al Gharbi Mountains to Ibri in the Dhahirah Region. In old geology the sedimentary rocks in this area were under the sea, which was known as the Hawasinah Ocean. The fortifications along this wadi reflect the rocky environment of the deep-ocean sediments on which they are built. Fortified houses as well as watchtowers are constructed of stone, which gives a dark brown colour to the structures, and a different texture from the usual mud-brick towers. The old stone towers have also survived the rigours of nature and time better than their mud-brick counterparts. Gheizen, set on a high bluff above the wadi bed, is the largest village on the wadi. Four towers remain at the corners of what was once a wall around the village. Several old cannon are lying around, and one still points from a tower port.

The stone fortifications of Al Majahjah (left) and Al Harmali (above and below) reflect the rocky environment of Wadi Hawasinah.

SOHAR

Looking at Sohar today, a small quiet village on the Gulf, it stretches one's imagination to see it as the capital of the country. But it was the capital on several occasions. Ibn Hawqal wrote in the 10th century: "Sohar is the capital and is on the sea. Its traders and commerce cannot be enumerated. It is the most developed and wealthy town in Oman. The rest of Islam hardly knows that a town such as Sohar with its wealth and development exists on the Persian Sea."

Sohar is believed to be the Omana of ancient Roman scholars, Pliny and Ptolemy. The site of Sohar has been specifically identified as a centre of a Nestorian bishopric as early as 424 AD. The sailors of Sohar traded throughout the Gulf and the Indian Ocean long before the advent of Islam. The first Muslim missions to Oman were warmly welcomed by the Julandas, the first Imams of Oman dating back to circa 751 AD.

The earliest fortress was discovered under the present fort by the Mission Archéologique Francaise à Bahrain et Oman in 1980. The first fort was built of baked bricks, surmounted by mud bricks, and was 45 metres long on each of its four sides, with a massive tower at each corner. There is no evidence that Oman had kilns for firing bricks, so the bricks may have originated in Persia. A date store, armoury, and arsenal were partly uncovered. The earliest fort dates to the 13th or early 14th century, and is attributed to the Princess of Hormuz.

When the Portuguese occupied the fortress in the 16th century, they reduced the boundary wall and replaced the old bricks with stone. Two towers were built on the shore side, one being destroyed 200 to 300 years ago and the other in 1982.

Sohar Fort was the centre of many conflicts. During one civil war, in 1724, the leaders of the two main tribes, Yamani and Naziri, were killed in the Battle of Sohar. The civil war continued until 1737 when Persian forces invaded Oman at Sohar. The Omani tribes united, ending their fratricidal war, to fight the Persians who were defeated at Sohar in 1744 by Imam Ahmed bin Said.

When several tribes, led by the Wahhabis, broke through the defences of the western Hajar passes in 1785, Sohar Fort was successfully defended against their attacks.

Today Sohar Fort reflects the importance of its past, when it was built to protect the town in her Golden Age. It is a grand structure with six towers, five round and one square, joined by walls four storeys high, overlooking the beach of Sohar.

WADI JIZZI

Wadi Jizzi runs through the northern range of the Hajar Al Gharbi, connecting the oasis of Buraimi and the Batinah Coast. Unlike Wadi Samail, there are few tower ruins along Wadi Jizzi.

The main towers to be seen today are at Al Hail (below), Al Rabi and Al Wasit, located about half-way between Sohar and Buraimi. Al Hail and Al Rabi are opposite each other on the wadi. Al Hail has two restored towers high above a wadi canyon near the Royal Oman Police checkpoint. Al Rabi's tower is perched on a pinnacle rock 60 metres high, but within shouting distance of a small restored fortlet. These towers were originally built by the

Persians preceding the introduction of Islam, when Persia controlled the Batinah Plain, and the Arabs controlled the interior and highlands. The outposts protected the maritime plain from bedu attacks. Two clans occupied Al Hail and were enemies of a clan in Al Wasit. Bitter quarrels escalated into free fights often ending in bloodshed. Al Hail villagers had the advantage of being able to obstruct the falaj water supply to the lower valley which usually brought a hasty termination to hostilities.

Al Wasit, a small village near Al Rabi, has a beautiful restored tower with an attached room. Its secondary defence is a restored tower on a nearby hill.

BURAIMI FORT

Buraimi was a large oasis with a collection of villages clustered about it, lying mid-way between Sohar on the Gulf of Oman and the Arabian Gulf. Its strategic position with abundant water sources, date groves and fruit trees, has made it a centre of conflict through the centuries. Today the oasis is divided into Buraimi in Oman territory and Al Ain in the United Arab Emirates.

It is thought that the original fort was built by the Al Bu Shamis, a division of the Na'im, the main tribe living in the area. It was occupied by the Wahhabis in the first part of the 19th century and strengthened by Mutlaq Al Mutairi, the Wahhabi naib (leader) between 1808 and 1813. He improved the fort's structure and built the formidable moat. The Wahhabis held the fort until 1839, when the Na'im tribe took it in their bid for independence.

In 1840, the British government sent Captain Atkins Hamerton to Buraimi to gather information about the region and its inhabitants. The following is from his report: "Brymee [Buraimi] is a town of considerable size, built of sun-dried mud bricks, and surrounded by a wall constructed of similar material, but the greater part of the town is represented to be in a dilapidated state, and the wall in perfect ruin. On the south side of the town, however, in an open plain, is a fort, nearly square, surrounded by a dry ditch [moat], about twenty-four feet wide, inside of which is a wall about eight feet high, for the protection of the matchlockmen while defending the ditch. About thirty feet distant, and inside this wall, is the fort wall, about fourteen feet in height and five in thickness at the base, and at the top only eighteen inches or two feet."

A brass cannon bearing the name of Said bin Sultan, now rests near the gate of the fort. It is believed to be one of 20 cannons purchased from America for the Sultan's corvette. In 1840, Hamerton discovered a similar gun at Burj Al Shujairi, on his way along Wadi Jizzi from Sohar to Buraimi. When he asked how it came to be there, it is said that he was told it had been sent by 'Seyyid Said' for installation in the main fort at Buraimi, but it could not be dragged beyond Burj Al Shujairi. Hamerton could not discover when it had been sent.

The fort buildings were restored during the 1980s by the Regional Development Council, using traditional techniques: mud bricks, saruj, palm logs and reed mat roofing material. A nearby large watchtower, part of the fort's outer defences, can be entered by climbing a rope dangling from an entrance half-way up the tower's side.

SHINAS FORT

Shinas Fort is the last fort on the coast of Oman before the United Arab Emirates border. The restored fort has the classic design of four walls forming a rectangle, with round towers at each corner. Entering through the gate, past beautiful massive doors, a visitor faces an open courtyard. Only mud-brick buttresses and foundations outline where rooms once stood against the walls. The Wali holds receptions in a majlis near the entrance.

The 18th-century inhabitants of Shinas enjoyed a prosperous sea trade and lived on fishing and agriculture. For a period around the 1800s, Shinas was under the protection of Persia. During this period the Wahhabis acted independently of the rest of Oman in various activities, one of which, with the Qasimi, was attacking British ships engaged in East India Company trade. As a result a combined Omani and British naval force took action.

Shinas Fort was caught up in this activity and on 1 January, 1810, was bombarded by a combined Omani and British force of ships and gunboats. The ships were too distant for the bombardment to be effective. Troops were landed the following day with a 10.5-inch mortar and two howitzers, which also proved ineffective. On the third day, when more cannons were moved from the ships – two 24-pounders and four 12-pounders – a breach was made in the wall. One tower fell in, but guns directed at the other towers failed to dislodge the defenders. Omani troops entered the breach and the fort surrendered.

MUSANDAM

The spectacular mountains of the Musandam Peninsula rise straight out of the sea to a height of 2,000 metres. Some have compared the beauty of Musandam's inlets with the fjords of Norway. 'Musandam' is an Arabic word for 'anvil', referring to the shape of the peninsula's northern headland which juts out into the sea, separating the Arabian Gulf from the Gulf of Oman and the Indian Ocean by the Strait of Hormuz. Khor Habalayn and Khor Al Shamm, the two main inlets, were frequently used as hiding places by 19th century Qasimi sailors after seafaring ventures. To elude pursuit they could retreat into these inlets whose entrances were hidden from the open sea.

During the early 1900s Musandam was technically Omani but the distance and isolation made it difficult to exercise much influence from Muscat. The local Shihuh tribe, one of the original inhabitants of the area, kept very much to themselves. The area remained in seclusion from the rest of Oman until 1970. Now mountain and coast roads make Musandam easily accessible, where not long ago travel to mountain villages was by foot or donkey. The tracks were too steep for camels. Even today some villages are accessible only by sea.

In the early 17th century a fort was built in Khasab by the Portuguese. The fort is located on the inner cove of Khasab Bay, a fine natural harbour 8 kilometres long and 5 kilometres wide. The fort is a square with four bastions connected by curtain walls.

In 1624 the Portuguese Admiral, Ruy Freire da Andrade, made it his base when attempting to recapture Hormuz, 88 kilometres across the Strait of Hormuz. It was his failure in this venture which led to Muscat becoming the Portuguese main base.

The fort at Bukha is on the Arabian Gulf side of Musandam. Built of stone, as are many forts in the jebels, its design differs from the conventional Omani fort (see Introduction). The square towers are at opposite corners with a large contoured round tower on the inland corner. Its low walls were made more inaccessible by a surrounding moat.

Bukha Fort (this page) and Khasab Fort (opposite) before and after renovation.

MUSCAT WATCHTOWERS

Watchtowers completed the defence system of old Muscat. The town wall protected the rear of the town, although the sheer ophiolite mountains surrounding the town were impregnable. On the bay side were Forts Mirani and Jalali. On a jetty at the bay entrance was Fort Shira and across the bay on an island were two watchtowers. From the mountain tops five burnt-umber towers formed a protective arc around Muscat.

On the other side of Muscat's mountains, Mutrah Fort commands Mina Qaboos Harbour. Nine restored towers surround its landward side. Buildings of the souq surround an old stone tower near the Luti enclave, Sur Al Luwatiya.

Within Metropolitan Muscat, which extends 50 kilometres from Muscat, are many palm-tree-lined wadis and small farms enclosed by giant mountains. Typical of this locale is Saal (below). Three watchtowers provided protection for the village in a terraced palm grove above a deep channel formed by erosion from the wadi. The central tower seems to have been part of a fortlet, indicated by a remaining stone foundation.

South east of Muscat is probably the most photographed tower in Oman. It is at Quriyat. At low tide the tower is accessible by foot. This restored triangular-shaped tower seems to emerge from conglomerate boulders atop a large yellow sand dune over tertiary rock (right). The tower is shown on a plan of Quriyat, dated 1635, as a secondary defence to the walled town, which no longer exists. Quriyat was one of the coastal towns that suffered atrocities at the hands of the Portuguese during their conquest in 1507. A rectangular single-tower fort is in the centre of the town. There is nothing unusual about it, unlike the famous watchtower on the outskirts of Quriyat.

SUR

To the east of Muscat lies the fortified city of Sur, an important trading centre with east Africa during Oman's Golden Age. Sur was the only town that collected customs duties on its extensive foreign trade. The fortified customs gate-house still stands. A coffee fleet operated from the port of Sur in the 1870s, but there is little information available about the coffee trade. Sur also had a large shipyard where the famous dhows and sambouqs were built.

A dominating fort, Fort Sinesilas was restored in 1989. It stands on a high knoll overlooking the town of Sur and is said to have been built 300 years ago. The interior has been restored, with the exception of the partial walls of a former room. It is a typical square fort with round towers at each of the four corners.

Three more forts made up the total defence system of Sur. The renovated Fort Bilad Sur, with its unusual tower, is surrounded by a palm grove in a part of Sur named Hesse. This fort provided defence against raiding tribes from the interior. Across an inlet, in Aiga, are the ruins of Fort Al Hamouda. A well-preserved entrance door is locked but a crumbled wall section permits entry into the fort. On a hill overlooking the inlet and the Sur dhow-building beaches lie the remains of a curved bastion made of stone and coral. The fort appears to have had many cannons, as several remain scattered on the ground near the ruins. Seven towers which formed a line on a plateau behind Aiga, and numerous other towers, created the outer defences of Sur.

Fort Sinesilas (opposite and below) and Fort Bilad Sur (above) form part of the extensive defence system of Sur.

WADI FULAIJ

Wadi Fulaij empties into the Arabian Gulf at Sur. At the other end of the wadi, Al Kamil and Al Wafi lie on the border of the Wahiba Sands. Over the centuries, each tribe along the wadi had to control its own water supply, land and livestock. Control was exercised by manning watchtowers and forts. Since the Omani Renaissance of 1970, old feuds have died, tribalism has diminished in favour of nationalism, and migration has dissolved old rivalries. Remaining are the ruins of old castles, forts with their dungeons, watchtowers, and walls surrounding towns. The walls around Al Kamil are unusually high.

Shaab lies east of Sur and is not along Wadi Fulaij but its uniqueness warrants mentioning here. The watchtower is among the buildings lining the top of a high tertiary-rock cliff overlooking a beautiful wadi. The village slopes down to a white sand beach on the Gulf of Oman.

Walls around Al Kamil (below) and Al Wafi (right) stand as reminders of old conflicts in Wadi Fulaij.

MUDAIRIB

On entering Mudairib, the visitor gets the impression that it is a town of towers. There are towers among fortified mansions, near old walled town ruins, next to new homes and topping the many ophiolite hills around the city.

Mudairib is fairly new compared to many Omani communities. It seems that in the middle of the 18th century AD, the inhabitants of Ibra felt confined in the area they were cultivating, and took advantage of the relative peace of the time to look for new lands. Some factions left Ibra and settled 20 kilometres to the south-east where a falaj surfaced in Mudairib.

There are ten buildings called sablas in Mudairib. The sabla, a term unique to Oman, is a meeting and reception room of a family group or faction. The men of the group meet here several times a day to discuss the latest news or topics, and in times of conflict, the sabla was also the fortified stronghold for its people .

The other main fortifications of Mudairib were three types of buildings used only for defence: the burj (tower), the dirwaza (fortified city gate), and the qal'a (fort).

A tower on the falaj, surrounded by houses in the oldest part of Mudairib, was restored in 1977. Other towers are placed at various city boundaries. Dirwazat Kisham is the only well-preserved gate in Mudairib. It is a rectangular tower whose lower part permits entry into the city from the north through a large carved door followed by a vestibule. Access to the upper part of the tower is by a ramp from an adjoining sabla. It is covered and has several loopholes for rifles and one for a small cannon. Wooden rungs in the wall lead to the roof terrace from which the battlements were manned.

A fort, to the east of the souq on the highest hill of Mudairib, was built by Abdullah bin Suleiman bin Mohammed of the Awlad Hamad faction. He died in 1842, which gives an idea of the fort's age. Three towers, two of which are in good condition, are joined by a stone wall now in ruins.

The fort of Khanajira overlooks the souq and the centre of the city. It consists of two parts – a large single tower which dominates the old part of Mudairib, and a tower attached to an L-shaped building.

In case of attack, each part of the city was defended by its own faction. Walls of towers or fortified homes were equipped for defence, with battlements, cannon holes, and rows of loopholes oriented in different directions.

Above the main doors of fortified structures there is a hole called a kuwwa, from which asal (boiling honey) or khall (hot oil) could be poured on enemies trying to breach the entrance.

The besieged inhabitants, who also had a supply of wood for casting lead bullets, prepared gunpowder in polished holes in a rock which can still be seen.

The exteriors and interiors of Omani houses are plain and undecorated, except for the ceilings. Palm-log beams are painted in a dark reddish-brown colour similar to burnt sienna. It is made from a rock extracted from a small hill south of Mudairib. In many houses, especially the sabla, ceiling motifs are often applied, ranging from simple geometric or floral designs to decoration equivalent to that of an oriental rug.

The architecture of Mudairib is influenced by Africa. Many of the residents spent many years in Zanzibar.

SHARQIYAH REGION

Some of the many villages on the flat plains of Sharqiyah were formerly enclosed within walls, and all had watchtowers. Towers abound in Al Wasil, and several can be seen rising above the palm groves which hide the village of Al Riddah. One large tower stands next to an open space surrounded by large shade trees in the centre of this village, and it is here that the male villagers sit in a big circle on mats when observing funerals.

There are many towers topping the ophiolite hills around the city of Mudairib.

Two of the many towers in the Sharqiyah Region can be seen at Al Wasil (left) and Mudairib (above).

BILAD BANI BU ALI

The walled town of Bilad Bani bu Ali, south of Sur, was headquarters for the Bani bu Ali, a fierce warlike tribe. In the early 1800s they allied themselves with the Wahhabis and proceeded to use any opportunity to ravage, raid and pillage the surrounding countryside. Also any ship sailing close to their port, Al Ashkhara, was fair game for them.

In 1820, an attack on an Indian merchant ship brought a letter of protest, delivered by representatives of the Sultan. They were murdered on landing at Al Ashkhara. This was followed by an attack by a British and Omani force in November, led by Captain Thompson, against the Bani bu Ali. The tribe counter-attacked with unexpected ferocity and won the battle.

A few months later, in March 1821, another British/Omani force under Major General Lionel Smith attacked Bilad Bani bu Ali with musketry and bayonets against a thousand desperate charging Bani bu Ali swordsmen. The British/Omani force was victorious, and rebellious activities ended. An eye-witness account of the battle was recorded by A. Chricton in *History of Arabia*, 1833:

"All who beheld this extraordinary attack concur in declaring that more determined courage and self-devoting resolution never was displayed by any men than by these Arabs. They defended their fortress with a bravery approaching to frenzy and not only were they totally unchecked in their advance by the heavy and well-sustained fire, which mowed them down in multitudes every instant; but despising the lines of bayonets opposed to them, they threw themselves upon the troops, seizing their weapons with both hands to break their ranks, and sacrificed themselves to cut down their enemies, even with the bayonet sticking in their bodies."

The huge fort at Bilad Bani bu Ali could protect thousands of people seeking refuge behind its walls during tribal warfare.

BILAD BANI BU HASAN

Near Bilad Bani bu Ali is Bilad Bani bu Hasan, another walled town with a very large fort. The mud walls are in disrepair but the fort has been restored. A lone cannon of 1790 vintage has been mounted in the courtyard. The walled town is surrounded by date palms and considerable farm land.

A visitor in 1845 arrived in Bilad Bani bu Hasan on the day that peace had been concluded between the Bani bu Hasan and the Bani bu Ali. The visitor witnessed about 50 men mounted on camels, fully equipped for war, arriving to ratify the agreement. It so happened that the next month would be Dhul-Haja, the month of Haj or pilgrimage, and peace between the two tribes would permit performing the pilgrimage unmolested. Usually, once Dhul-Haja had elapsed, the war was renewed as before.

British and Omani troops assembled in Bilad Bani bu Hasan in 1821 before attacking Bilad Bani bu Ali.

MARBAT

A fort in the incense port of Marbat, near Salalah, was the site of a battle which was a milestone in the Dhofar War, a communist armed insurrection (1971-1976). It was probably the last battle in the world involving conventional attack and defence of a fort.

At dawn on 19 July, 1972, a large rebel force, about 250 strong, attacked the port of Marbat in the Dhofar province of southern Oman. An eyewitness to the battle, Colonel Tony Jeapes, wrote in his book *SAS: Operation Oman*: "...The adoo (enemy) had never attacked with this intensity before... At a signal, the men started to run in an extended line, raising their weapons to their shoulders. The crackle of small arms fire sounded paltry against the ear-splitting noise of bursting shells... As if it was a signal to begin, the whole corner near the fort erupted with the sound of machine guns and rifles mixed with the explosion of shells. All the enemy's fire seemed to be directed at the fort...as it disappeared from sight in a cloud of brown smoke and dust."

When the battle started Corporal Labalaba and Trooper Takavesi, both members of a nine-man Special Air Service Action Team, went to man a 25-pounder gun just outside the walls of the fort. Gunner Walid Khalfan of the Oman Artillery was already there. It immediately became clear that the main enemy thrust was being directed against the fort, and in particular against the gun which was firing at point blank range. Before long the entire crew was wounded. Captain Kealy, the Commander of the SAS detachment, and Trooper Tobin, who was a trained medical orderly, then ran under fire from the main SAS position to help save the gun. The rebels continued to attack with great ferocity and made repeated attempts to take the gun, often within grenade-throwing range. The action lasted nearly four hours before a relief force and an accompanying air strike drove off the enemy. During this action Corporal Labalaba and Trooper Tobin were killed and Trooper Takevesi and Gunner Walid Khalfan both seriously wounded.

The official report records that the fate of Marbat and its occupants during the battle depended on the action of these nine men. Without their resolve the town of Marbat would have fallen.

There are two forts in Marbat. One is the Wali's fort (right) built along the beach by Mohammed Akil in 1806. The other, the Dhofar Gendarmerie fort where the battle took place, was built on a hill above the Wali's fort, by Seyyid Turki in 1880.

MISCELLANY

FORT INFLUENCES

Once a visitor to Oman has seen its forts, there is an awareness that fort influence pervades the country's architecture both in private homes and in public buildings. There are large main entry gates in walls surrounding houses; and variations on watchtowers, crenellations and gun slots in the buildings themselves. Plaques illustrating forts have been placed along the Corniche in Mutrah (below) and a monument to forts built on a roundabout at Seeb near Muscat (right). Five denominations of Omani currency and twenty-six postage stamps also feature forts.

The similarity between the design of forts and of domestic houses is not the result of builders' whims. It is because the characteristics of Omani architecture have evolved from the fort, which was the centre of the community and a symbol of power for its occupants. Most large houses were built with defence as a major factor and so homes were related to a military prototype.

In most Omani buildings, decorative elements are secondary to the strength and size of the very solid-looking main structure. This reflects the martial aspect of life as it was in the past in Oman and is in complete contrast to many other Islamic countries where the application of decoration to domestic architecture has resulted in the dominance of purely decorative geometrical filigree designs. However buildings in the Sur area do reflect this decorative style, possibly from African influence. Elsewhere the civil architecture seems to be based, in a reduced scale, on the forts and castles, giving an overall effect of a unified national architectural style.

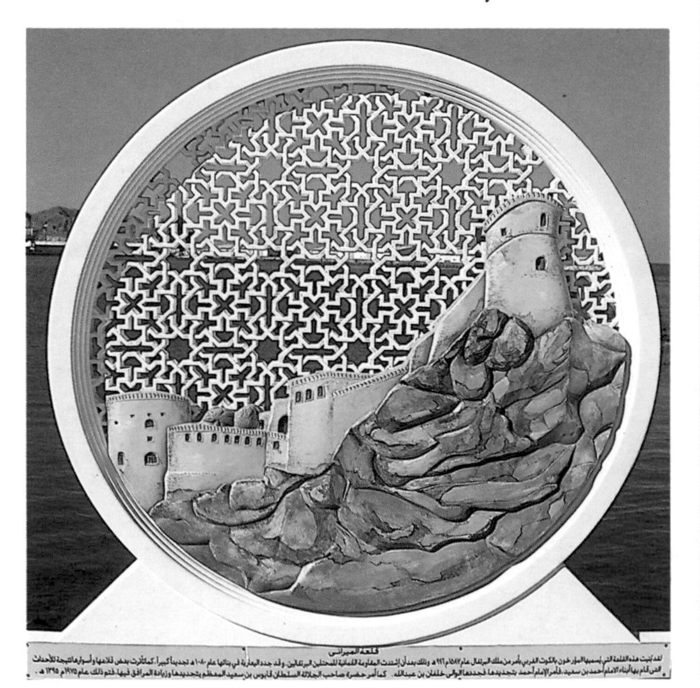

GLOSSARY

adoo: enemy
anf al-bab: the centre wood strip which overlaps the joint of large Omani doors
asgailee (assaiqali): sword
askari: East African native soldier or policeman
bab: main gate
bani: tribal prefix meaning 'the sons of'
barasti: a house of palm wood and frond construction
barbican: the outer defence of a city or castle, especially a double tower above a gate or drawbridge
badawi (pl. bedu): desert nomads
burj: tower
corvette: a flush-decked warship with one tier of guns
dirwaza: fortified city gate
dishdasha: long Arab shirt, principal male garment
dhow: general term for Arab sailing vessels with lanteen rigging
Dhul-Haj: the month of Haj (see below)
falaj: irrigation channel
fardha: access point to a falaj
ghafir (pl. ghafar): protector or guide
guard tower: fortified tower separate from a fort, although some had an attached room, becoming a fortlet
Haj: pilgrimage to Mecca and the other holy places, incumbent upon every Muslim
halwa: sweetmeat made of starch, brown sugar, ghee and almonds
hisn: large rectangular enclosure
Imam: spiritual and secular leader of the people
jebel: mountain or mountain range
joos: compound of fired mud
khanjar: curved dagger in elaborate silver sheath; part of the formal Omani dress
kuwwa/machicolation: a space between the corbels (projections of stone or timber) supporting a parapet, or an opening in the floor of a projecting gallery, from which solids and liquids were dropped on an attacking enemy
loophole: opening in the wall of a fortification that flares outwards
majlis: reception room, where men receive their visitors and guests
mihrab: recess in a wall facing in the direction of Mecca
ogee arch: an arch with two continuous s-shaped curves meeting at the apex
qahwa: coffee
qal'a: fort
qarn: small hill
sabla: Omani meeting and reception room for a family group
sambouq: large type of sailing boat used for cargo
saruj: a local Omani cement-mixture of baked lime and mud
souq: market.
sur (pl. aswar): fortified walled area
wadi: a valley; also the river that may or may not be running at the bottom of a valley
Wahhabism: the form of Islam deriving from the doctrine of Mohammed bin Abdul Wahhab
Wali: district governor
zajarah: animal-powered wells

RULERS OF OMAN

rule began	
AD	*Julandas Dynasty*
751	Julanda bin Mas'ud
—	Mohammed bin Affan
801	Warith bin Kaab
807	Ghassan bin Abdulla
824	Abdul Malik bin Hamad
840	Al Muhanna bin Jaifar
851	Al Salt bin Malik
886	Rashid bin An Nadhr
890	Azzan bin Tamim
897	Mohammed bin Al Hasan
898	Azzan bin Al Hizr
899	Abdulla bin Mohammed
900	Al Salt bin Al Qasim
900	Hasan bin Said
904	Al Hawari bin Matraf
912	Omar bin Mohammed
—	Mohammed bin Yazid
—	Mullah Al Bahari
939	Said bin Abdulla
—	Rashid bin Walid
1009	Al Khalil bin Shadzan
1053	Rashid bin Said
1053	Hafs bin Rashid
1054	Rashid bin Ali
1154 ?	bin Jabir Musa
	Nebhani Period
1154	Al Fallah bin Al Muhsin
—	Arar bin Fallah
—	Mudhaffar bin Suleiman
—	Makhzum bin Al Fallah
1406	Malik bin Ali
	Imams
1435	Abu'l Hasan
1451	Omar bin Al Khattab
1490	Omar Al Sharif
—	Ahmed bin Mohammed
1500	Mohammmed bin Ismail
1529	Barakat bin Muhammed
1560	Abdulla bin Mohammed
	Ya'ruba Dynasty
1624	Nasir bin Murshid
1649	Sultan bin Saif I
1688	Bil'arub bin Sultan
1692	Saif bin Sultan I
1711	Sultan bin Saif II
1718	Saif bin Sultan II
1718	Muhanna bin Sultan
1721	Ya'rub bin Bil'arub
1722	Saif bin Sultan II
1724	Mohammed bin Nasir
1728	Saif bin Sultan II
1738	Sultan bin Murshid
	Al Bu Said Dynasty
1741	Ahmed bin Said
1783	Said bin Ahmed
	Seyyids and Sultans
1779	Hamad bin Said
1792	Sultan bin Ahmed
1804	Said bin Sultan
1856	Thuwaini bin Said
1866	Salim bin Thuwaini
1868	Azzan bin Qais
1871	Turki bin Said
1888	Faisal bin Turki
1913	Taimur bin Faisal
1932	Said bin Taimur
1970	Qaboos bin Said

SUR FLOOR PLANS

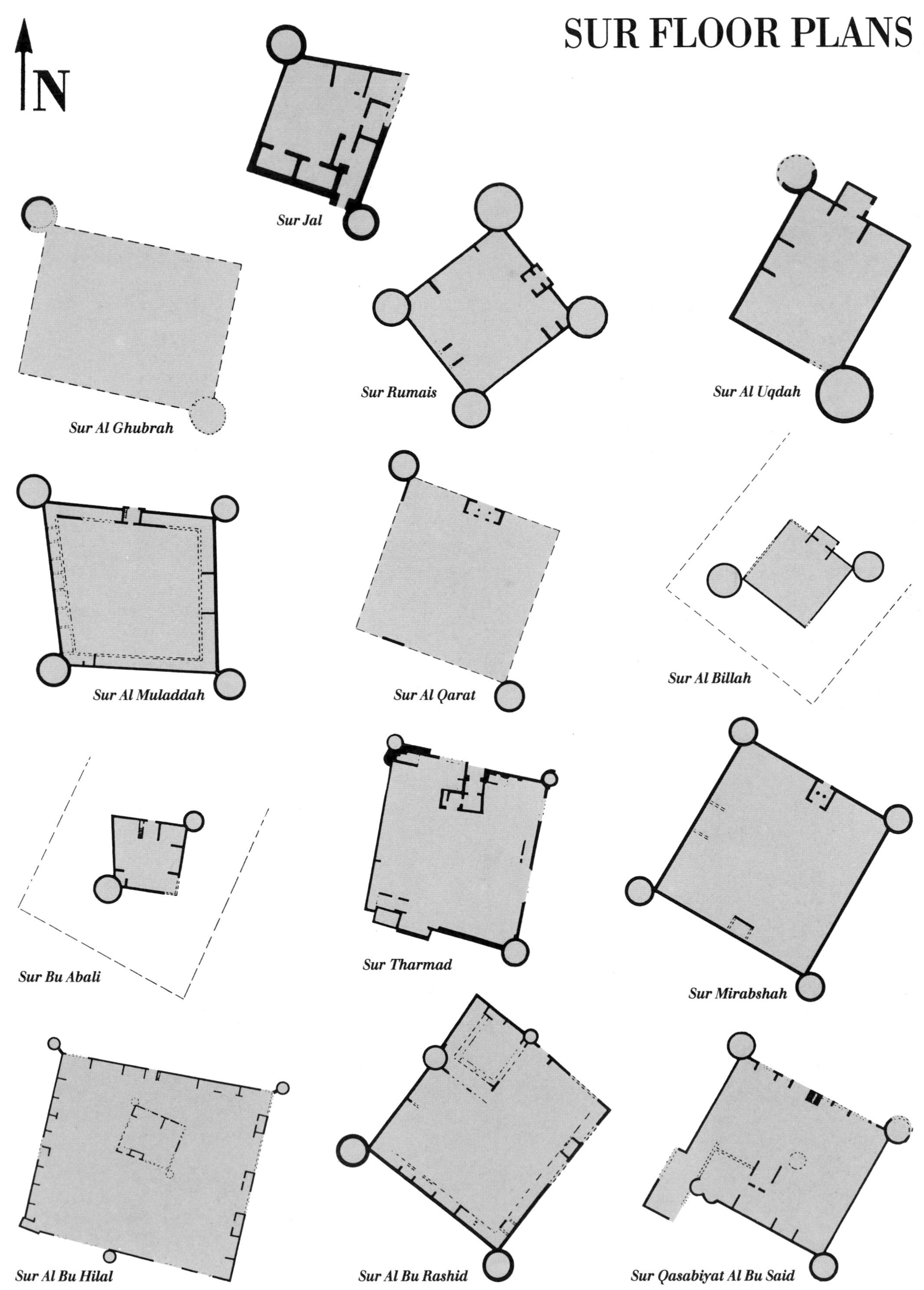

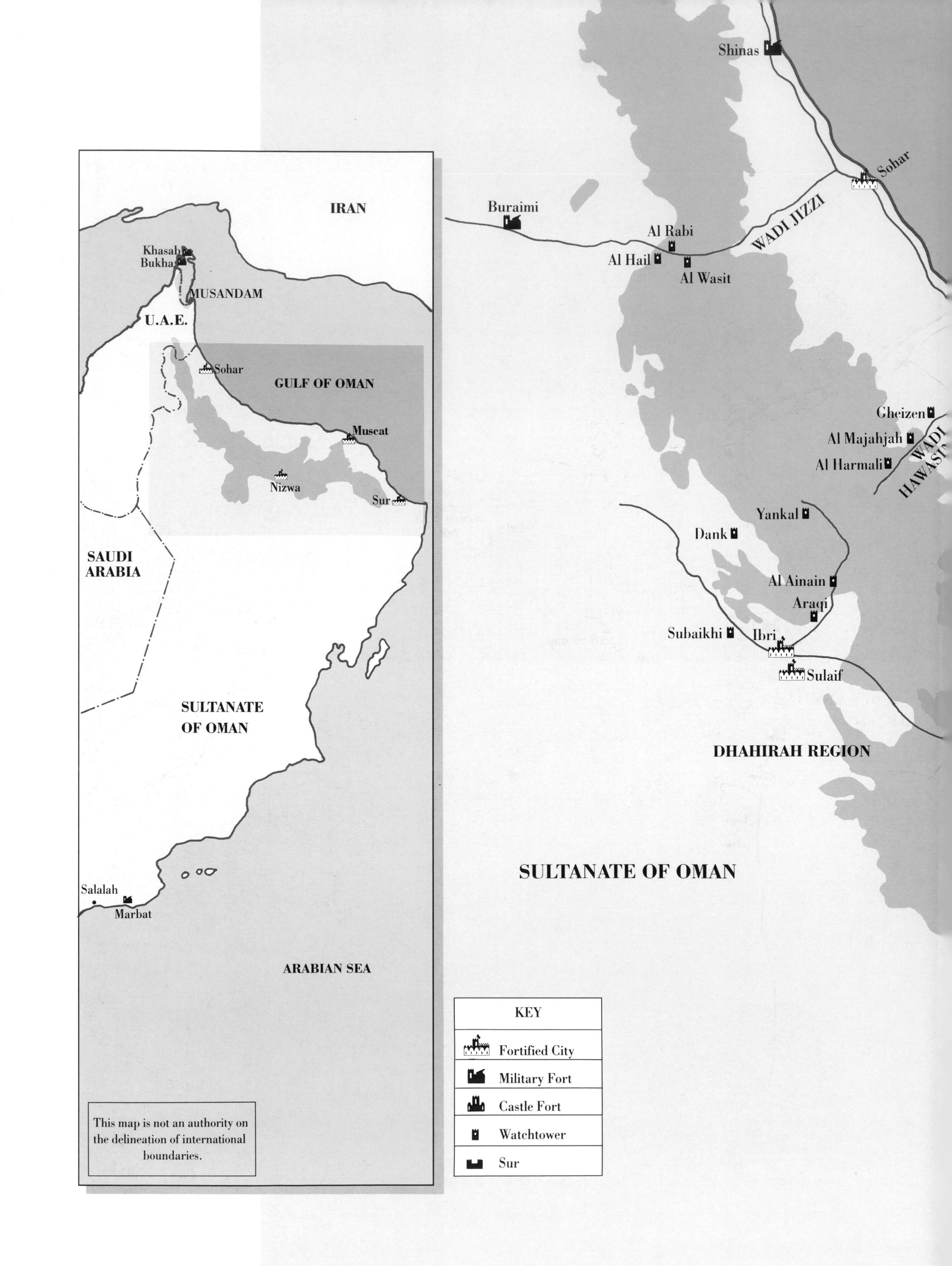

IRAN
Khasab
Bukha
MUSANDAM
U.A.E.
Sohar
GULF OF OMAN
Muscat
Nizwa
Sur
SAUDI
ARABIA
SULTANATE
OF OMAN
Salalah
Marbat
ARABIAN SEA
This map is not an authority on the delineation of international boundaries.
Shinas
Sohar
Buraimi
Al Rabi
WADI JIZZI
Al Hail
Al Wasit
Gheizen
Al Majahjah
WADI
HAWASIN
Al Harmali
Yankal
Dank
Al Ainain
Araqi
Subaikhi
Ibri
Sulaif
DHAHIRAH REGION
SULTANATE OF OMAN
KEY
Fortified City
Military Fort
Castle Fort
Watchtower
Sur

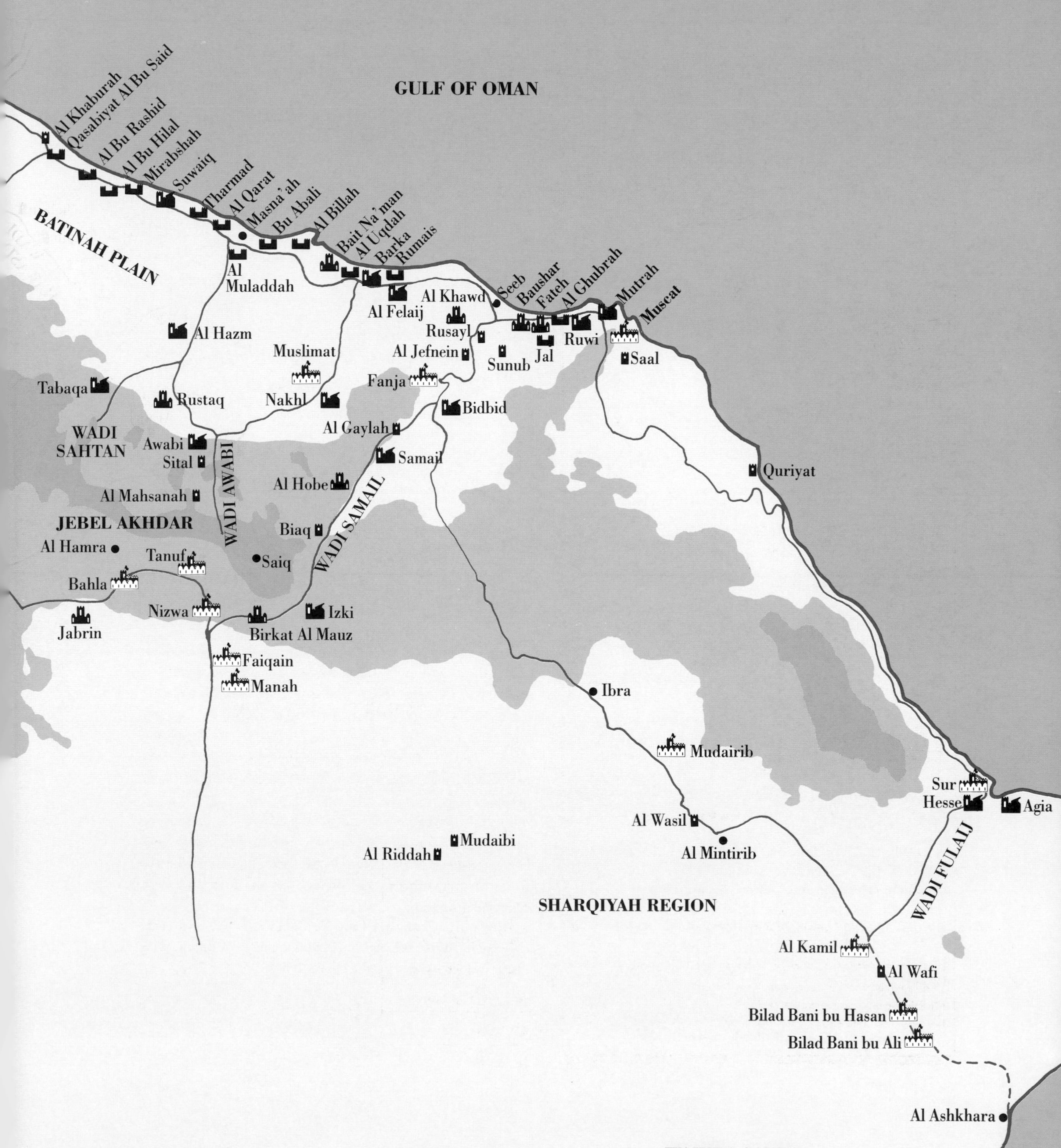

GULF OF OMAN
Al Khaburah
Qasabiyat Al Bu Said
Al Bu Rashid
Al Bu Hilal
Mirabshah
Suwaiq
Tharmad
Al Qarat
Masna'ah
Bu Abali
Al Billah
Bait Na'man
Al Uqdah
Barka
Rumais
BATINAH PLAIN
Al Muladdah
Al Felaij
Al Khawd
Seeb
Baushar
Fateh
Al Ghubrah
Mutrah
Muscat
Al Hazm
Muslimat
Rusayl
Al Jefnein
Sunub
Jal
Ruwi
Saal
Tabaqa
Rustaq
Nakhl
Fanja
Bidbid
WADI SAHTAN
Awabi
Sital
Al Gaylah
Samail
Quriyat
Al Mahsanah
Al Hobe
WADI AWABI
WADI SAMAIL
JEBEL AKHDAR
Biaq
Al Hamra
Tanuf
Saiq
Bahla
Nizwa
Izki
Jabrin
Birkat Al Mauz
Faiqain
Manah
Ibra
Mudairib
Sur
Hesse
Agia
Al Wasil
Al Mintirib
Mudaibi
Al Riddah
SHARQIYAH REGION
WADI FULAIJ
Al Kamil
Al Wafi
Bilad Bani bu Hasan
Bilad Bani bu Ali
Al Ashkhara
WAHIBA SANDS

BIBLIOGRAPHY

Al Qasimi, M., *The Myth of Arab Piracy in the Gulf*, Croom Helm, London, 1985

Bonnenfant, P. and G. and Salim ibn Hamad ibn Sulayman Al Harthi, 'Architecture and Social History at Mudayrib', *Journal of Oman Studies*, Vol. 3, Part 2, Ministry of National Heritage and Culture, Oman, 1977

Costa, Dr Paolo, 'Bayt Naman, a 17th Century Mansion of the Batinah' and 'The Sur of the Batinah', *Journal of Oman Studies*, Vol. 8, Ministry of National Heritage and Culture, Oman, 1985

d'Erico, E., 'Introduction to Oman. Military Architecture of the Late 16th, 17th and 18th Centuries', *Journal of Oman Studies*, Vol. 6, Ministry of National Heritage and Culture, Oman, 1983

Duchess of St. Albans, *Where Time Stood Still: A Portrait of Oman*, Quartet Books, London, 1980

Galderi, E., 'Masterpiece of Omani 17th Century Architecture', *Journal of Oman Studies*, Vol. 1, Ministry of National Heritage and Culture, Oman, 1975

Graz, L., *The Omanis: Sentinels of the Gulf*, Longman, London, 1982

Hamilton, Alexander, *A New Account of the East Indies (1688-1723)*, Argonaunt Press, 1930

Hawley, Sir Donald, *Oman and its Renaissance*, Stacey International, London, 1977

Hill, A. and Hill, D., *The Sultanate of Oman*, Longman, London, 1977

Jeapes, Colonel Tony, *SAS: Operation Oman*, W. Kimbar, London, 1980

Kay, Shirley, *Enchanting Oman*, Motivate Publishing, Dubai, 1988

Kelly, J.B., *Britain and the Persian Gulf*, Oxford University Press, London, 1968

Marshall, B., 'The Journeys of S.B. Miles in Oman between 1885 and 1895', *Journal of Oman Studies*, Vol. 10, Ministry of National Heritage and Culture, Oman, 1975

Peyton, W., *Old Oman*, Stacey International, London, 1983

Phillips, Wendel, *Oman: A History*, Librairie Du Liban, Beirut, 1971

Richmond, Robert, 'Jabrin Restored', *A Tribute to Oman: National Day 1983*, Apex Publishing, Oman, 1983

Richmond, Robert, 'Oman's Splendid Forts' and 'Jabrin - Restored to Glory', *A Tribute to Oman: National Day 1985*, Apex Publishing, Oman, 1985

Richmond, Robert, 'Forts of Oman', *A Tribute to Oman: National Day 1986*, Apex Publishing, Oman, 1986

Risso, P., *Oman and Muscat: An Early Modern History*, Croom Helm, London, 1986

Sirhan, Sirhan bin Sa'id bin (E.C. Ross, trans.), *Annals of Oman to 1728*, Oleander Press, 1984

Skeet, I., *Oman Before 1970: The End of an Era*, Faber & Faber, London, 1974

Stevens, Andre, *Oman, Citadels Between Land and Sea*, Terra Incognito, Winksele, Belgium, 1990

Sultan's Armed Forces Museum, Bait Al Falaj, 'A Fort Reborn', *A Tribute to Oman: National Day 1985*, Apex Publishing, Oman, 1985

Ward, P., *Travels in Oman: On the Track of Early Explorers*, Oleander Press, 1987

Oman, A Seafaring Nation, Ministry of National Heritage and Culture, Muscat, Oman, 1979

Sultanate of Oman and Roads to Progress, Ministry of National Heritage and Culture, Oman, 1986

ACKNOWLEDGEMENTS

I extend special thanks to the Ministry of National Heritage and Culture and to Moral Guidance and Public Relations, Ministry of Defence, Oman. I also thank Charles Backhouse for his early editing advice, Gussan Al Jamali for braving wadis and jebels with me in search of fort ruins, the families Al Hina'i and Al Rawahi for their interviews and all the wonderful Omani people who permitted me to invade their privacy with my camera.

Special thanks are extended to Motivate Publishing, to Chuck Grieve for pointing the way and to Ann Verbeek for her editing task. Many thanks to Dick Zimmer and Julia Roles for providing recent pictures of the forts in Sohar, Bukha and Khasab.

Above all, to Desert Line Projects L.L.C., and their Chairman, Sheikh Ahmed Farid Mohammed Al Aulaqi, a big thank you for sponsoring the book.

INDEX

THE ARABIAN HERITAGE SERIES

Arabian Profiles
edited by Ian Fairservice
and Chuck Grieve

Land of the Emirates
by Shirley Kay

Enchanting Oman
by Shirley Kay

Bahrain — Island Heritage
by Shirley Kay

Dubai — Gateway to the Gulf
edited by Ian Fairservice

Abu Dhabi — Garden City of the Gulf
by Peter Hellyer
and Ian Fairservice

Fujairah — An Arabian Jewel
by Peter Hellyer

Portrait of Ras Al Khaimah
by Shirley Kay

Sharjah — Heritage and Progress
by Shirley Kay

Architectural Heritage of the Gulf
by Shirley Kay
and Dariush Zandi

Emirates Archaeological Heritage
by Shirley Kay

Seafarers of the Gulf
by Shirley Kay

Gulf Landscapes
by Elizabeth Collas
and Andrew Taylor

Birds of Southern Arabia
by Dave Robinson
and Adrian Chapman

Mammals of the Southern Gulf
by Christian Gross

The Living Desert
by Marycke Jongbloed

Seashells of Southern Arabia
by Donald and Eloise Bosch

The Living Seas
by Frances Dipper
and Tony Woodward

Sketchbook Arabia
by Margaret Henderson

The Thesiger Collection
a catalogue of unique photographs
by Wilfred Thesiger

Thesiger's Return
by Peter Clark
Black and white photography
by Wilfred Thesiger

Juha — Last of the Errant Knights
by Mustapha Kamal,
translated by Jack Briggs

Fun in the Emirates
by Aisha Bowers
and Leslie P. Engelland

Mother Without a Mask
by Patricia Holton

Library boxes and boxed sets are also available

Arabian Albums

Dubai An Arabian Album
by Ronald Codrai

Abu Dhabi An Arabian Album
by Ronald Codrai

Premier Editions

A Day Above Oman
by John Nowell

Forts of Oman
by Walter Dinteman

Land of the Emirates
by Shirley Kay

Enchanting Oman
by Shirley Kay

Abu Dhabi — Garden City of the Gulf
edited by Ian Fairservice
and Peter Hellyer

Arabian Heritage Guides

Snorkelling and Diving in Oman
by Rod Salm and Robert Baldwin

The Green Guide to the Emirates
by Marycke Jongbloed

Off-Road in the Emirates
by Dariush Zandi

Off-Road in Oman
by Heiner Klein
and Rebecca Brickson